Long-Term Change

in a

Quick-Fix World

Other Books by the Author

Beyond Leadership to Destiny*: Jacob's Lifetime Journey with God*
An Evangelical's Road Less Traveled*: A Contemplative Life*
Dying to Live*: The Christian's Pathway to Experiencing God More Deeply*
Praise in the Time Stream of Our Lives*: Wisdom from Starbucks and Other Vantage Points*

Long-Term Change
in a
Quick-Fix World

CHARLES HALEY

Wheaton, Illinois

© 2014 by Charles Haley

All rights reserved. No part of this publication may be reproduced, stored in a retrieval system, or transmitted in any way by any means—electronic, mechanical, photocopy, recording, or otherwise—without the prior permission of the copyright holder, except as provided by USA copyright law.

DISCLAIMER: In some cases personal names used in this book have been changed to protect privacy.

Unless otherwise indicated, Scripture quotations are from the New American Standard Bible®, copyright © 1960, 1962, 1963, 1968, 1971, 1972, 1973, 1975, 1977, 1995 by The Lockman Foundation. Used by permission.

Scripture quotations labeled KJV are from the King James Version.

Scripture quotations labeled NIV are taken from the Holy Bible, New International Version®, NIV®. Copyright © 1973, 1978, 1984, 2011 by Biblica, Inc.™ Used by permission of Zondervan. All rights reserved worldwide. www.zondervan.com. The "NIV" and "New International Version" are trademarks registered in the United States Patent and Trademark Office by Biblica, Inc.™

Italics in Scripture quotations indicate emphasis added by the author.

Material was taken and adapted with permission from the following works by the author:

In chapter 12: Charles Haley, "The Gospels and the Principle of Planting," chapter 1 in *Dying to Live: The Christian's Pathway to Experiencing God More Deeply* (Charleston, SC: CreateSpace, 2009).

In chapter 15: Charles Haley, "The Bible," part 11 in *Praise in the Time Stream of Our Lives: Wisdom from Starbucks and Other Vantage Points* (Wheaton: Life Serve, 2009).

In chapter 17: Charles Haley, "Meditation: The Timeless Discipline," chapter 12 in *An Evangelical's Road Less Traveled: A Contemplative Life* (Enamclaw, WA: Pleasant Word, 2009).

In chapter 23: Charles Haley, "Peniel—Crisis Transformation," chapter 10 in *Beyond Leadership to Destiny: Jacob's Lifetime Journey with God* (Wheaton: Life Serve, 2005).

In chapter 23, Charles Haley, "The Contemplative Process: Infused Meditation," chapter 19 in *An Evangelical's Road Less Traveled: A Contemplative Life* (Enamclaw, WA: Pleasant Word, 2009).

ISBN-13: 978-1-5025-1043-3
ISBN-10: 1-5025-1043-X

Life Serve
1825 College Avenue, Suite 130
Wheaton, Illinois 60187-4480
www.lifeserveltd.com

Cover design: Jason Bremer
Interior design and typesetting: CreateSpace Design Team
Editing: Carole Streeter

18 17 16 15 14 / 1 2 3 4 5 6 7 8 9 10

Printed in the United States of America

To Jo Ann, children, spouses, and families and the wide circle of those who are meaning-givers to me.

And to every new or young believer, serious Christian, small group member or seeker who engages with this book. Or, more simply, to each person who permits me to contribute something to your life, however small.

Contents

	Preface	xiii
	Acknowledgments	xv

Part 1: A Long Journey Required for Us All

1	Long-Term Change in a Quick-Fix World	5
2	Complexity: A Constant!	8
3	Long-Term Change: Barriers and Roadblocks	13
4	Long-Term Change: Culmination	17

Part 2: Long-Term Change: We Are Not Alone

5	The New Birth	23
6	God's Master Plan	27
7	The Bible	31
8	The Ministry of the Holy Spirit	34
9	Long-Term Change Together: The Church	41
10	Getting Pruned	47

Part 3: It's Up to Us: What We Do and How We Cooperate

11	Working It Out: What Is Up to Us?	54
12	Long-Term Changes in Stages: Falling Upward	62
13	Time to Grow Up: The X Factor	67
14	Sustained Relationship Over the Long Haul	72
15	The Bible: Using It!	77
16	Spiritual Disciplines	84
17	Meditation: The Timeless Discipline	91
18	The Promises!	96
19	Prayer: Foundation of Christian Experience	101
20	Habits of Holiness	107
21	The Mind Matters	113
22	Suffering and Affliction: Building Blocks Nobody Wants	121
23	Crisis Transformation	126
24	Healing: What Is Holding Us Back?	133

Part 4: How the Future Impacts Our Present

25	Kingdom Hope	141
26	Anticipating the Coming	146
	Conclusion: A Big Picture of Long-Term Change	151
	Bibliography	157
	About the Author	161
	About Life Serve	163

Preface

A *vision* should drive a book and a *commission* a Christian one. My *vision* for this work and hopefully *commission* too is to write an incisive, strategic, and distinctive book for this day that gives a broad view of the Christian life and provides value to

- Younger and older believers who desire a foundational source for the Christian life, not a Christian formula
- Members of small groups who want to dig into a resource that will contribute to transformation together . . . for the rest of their lives
- The occasional believer from a culture far removed from my Western one who will impact his or her culture far more than I do mine

One note of explanation in regard to format is that this book includes parenthetical in-text citations rather than footnotes or endnotes, plus a bibliography included at the back.

Acknowledgments

For me, relationships that last and are deepened along the way are a gift. I see beyond them to the Lord Himself. This week I happened to look in a project file for a previous book. A surprise greeted me! It was a piece of correspondence dated January 9, 1989, from Carole Streeter, who was working then as an acquisitions editor for a major Christian publisher. Along with Carole, more recent and deeply appreciated people who are gifts to this project are Paul Brinkerhoff, Wendell Hawley, and Sr. Mary Sharon Riley. Your input was critical for whatever this book turns out to be, but each of you is more to me than your valuable contributions.

Part I

A Long Journey Required for Us All

I remember Jack. He graduated ahead of me at the University of Illinois. He was headed for the ministry and was a meaningful member of our InterVarsity group. He became an avid student of ancient literature, which he read in classical Greek, and developed a passion for Greek philosophy. I heard news of him some time after graduation. He was contemplating suicide! Why? The report was that the power of Greek philosophy overruled the realities of life with God.

My encounter with Bo occurred years later in Fayetteville, North Carolina, when we moved there primarily to work with paratroopers from the 82nd Airborne Division in Fort Bragg. He is the only one of the many paratroopers we served that I remember vividly. Why? He was so spiritually hungry and could hardly get enough Bible study. I followed him over the years and kept his letters. He married a German woman and they were missionaries in Germany. We visited them on a trip there and saw the hole that Napoleon's troops blasted in the Heidelberg Castle fortification.

He developed a hobby of buying and selling antiques. He met a woman through this business. He divorced his wife and became a professional antique dealer. His life as an earnest follower of Christ seems to be lost permanently.

Discouraging truth about this phenomenon of falling along the way and failing to persevere is presented in our Lord's parables. One category asserts that "this is the man who hears the word and immediately receives it with joy; yet he has no firm root in himself, but is only temporary, and when affliction or persecution arises because of the word, immediately he falls away" (Matt. 13:20–21).

Steve Farrar in his book *Finishing Strong: Going the Distance for Your Family* (Sisters, OR: Multnomah, 1995) details this distasteful if not tragic phenomena of Christians *falling away* in large numbers and high percentages. According to his statistics, the majority of those who start well don't finish well.

Farrar quotes Dr. Paul Beck's warning to his future son-in-law, John Bisagno, who later became pastor of the First Baptist Church of Houston. "It has been my observation that just one out of ten who start out in full-time service for the Lord at twenty-one are still on track by the age of sixty-five. They're shot down morally, they're shot down with discouragement, they're shot down with liberal theology, they get obsessed with making money . . . but for one reason or another nine out of ten fall out" (6).

The twenty-year-old Bisagno didn't want to believe this. However, he wrote the names in the back of his Bible of twenty-four outstanding peers who were sold out to the Savior and committed preachers. Bisagno, with a sad heart, said eventually, "I am now fifty-three years old. From time to time as the years have gone by, I've had to turn back to that page in my

Bible and cross out a name. I wrote down those twenty-four names when I was just twenty years of age. Thirty-three years later, there are only *three* names remaining of the original twenty-four" (6).

Why is it that so many of us don't make it to the finish line? How can we fail to love our Lord all the way to the end? Even though the Christian life is hard, shouldn't we find the resources to pursue life with God through all our sufferings, heartbreaks and everything else to a victorious end of life?

Farrar drives the point further: "What makes you think you will be the one man out of ten who finishes strong? What makes you think that you won't be one of the nine who fall short of the mark? . . . When it comes to finishing strong the odds are against you. Finishing strong is not impossible. It is, however, improbable. It's going to take some tough choices and an experience or two of personal brokenness in order to have a strong finishing kick when you hit the tape at age sixty-five, seventy-five, eighty-five, or whenever it is that God calls you home" (8).

Does anyone have all the answers to this Christian life conundrum? My task in this book is not to solve every mystery of why Christians live successfully or fail miserably. My aim is to provide a broad approach to the Christian life—hopefully a valuable and strategic contribution that will give you a little better foothold on what makes up a life that will win the prize.

This is where we begin and will end. You will add your own touch according to how you understand what the Bible says about the Christian life. Your own experience may push you in a little different direction than what I take. But, it is the whole mosaic, not the parts, that dominates this tour of the Christian life. My prayer is for a long-term impact on each of our lives as we focus on *long-term change in a quick-fix world.*

1

Long-Term Change in a Quick-Fix World

Can you remember far enough back when you wrote a letter by hand to someone in a foreign country? Did you use a light-weight rice paper folding envelope? You would have labored to get your letter on its limited space, writing on all the flaps. Now, you talk for an hour with your contact—maybe in India, China or London while driving in your car! You can leave your map at home when you travel today—just use your GPS.

Jo Ann made a hotel reservation for us less than a hundred miles away. The reservationist for the transaction was in India! Making a phone call on your land line takes too long—text or e-mail! Did you ever get out of the car to open the garage door for Mom? Today you just push the button on the garage door opener you have in the car. Did Dad keep a tire gauge in the car when you were growing up? Now, just look on the console readout for all four tires while you are driving. Would you like to know what the weather is like in Tokyo? Find out on your cell phone.

A quick-fix mentality is deeply embedded in the way we think and live. The term *quick fix* is a slang expression that denotes an expedient solution to a problem, which is often temporary and unsatisfactory because it merely postpones having to deal with an overall problem. It's not a real fix, just a quick fix. Have you asked if our quality of life has been improved by a 4G lifestyle, let alone 5G and beyond? Is your web service faster than your friends', or is this significant anyway? What is the point of asking these questions in a book about *long-term change in a nanosecond world?*

A quick-fix mentality affects our thinking about living with God. Hundreds of books give us keys, facets or formulas on how we can live the Christian life successfully. Many can be powerfully helpful resources which reward the effort to read them and practice their message. You would have your classics as I do mine. One of my most meaningful is *The Return of the Prodigal Son* by Henri Nouwen. During my first days as a Christian, *Hudson Taylor's Spiritual Secret* stood out above the rest. For Jo Ann and me as a married couple, Harville Hendrix's *Getting the Love You Want: A Guide for Couples* tops the list.

However, we need balance! One size does not fill all our needs. Look at what the Bible says about the Christian life. *Long-term change is long term.* This can hardly be over emphasized in our quick-fix world. And, to be expected, our one task in this book is exploring the big picture—the long-term nature and the lifelong road of the Christian life. Hopefully we will find *rare air* in this hard climb.

So then, our instant, quick-fix, high-tech, 4G digital world too often sets the tone for our expectation regarding the life changes we want and seek. Our thirst, our frustrations about how to gain the changes we know we need, and repeated falls and failures, guarantee sales for this steady stream of books to help us along in our journeys. Use them, seek them out and keep reading! We also need the big picture to see how change occurs for us as Christians—*long-term change for the long run.*

The primary value of this book is not in the completeness of the treatment but in the power of the idea! Sixth-century St. Columba said something to this effect, "Pay little attention to my words, they are crude and of little import. Pay attention to the reality behind them." It is the power of how a life with God is presented in its many components from Old to New Testaments that is of value. We are involved in a life not primarily found in formulas, quick fixes or single ideas. We live in a complex world and our lives are too. While we might like everything in our Christian experience to be simple, neatly manageable, or easily understood, it's not the way our journeys work. We are exploring the process and taking the long view.

For Reflection and Discussion

1. Have you ever been surprised or perplexed about how difficult long-term change has been for you?
2. Have you found a particular approach or formula for Christian living that has been effective over a period of time? If so, describe it briefly.
3. How confident are you that you will experience the long-term change that you really want?
4. What would you like this book to contribute to you?

2

Complexity

A Constant!

Is the Christian life complex like everything around us and the universe in general? If it's not supposed to be rocket science, is it intended to be simple like a kindergarten picture or primitive like cave art?

The complexity of what we take for granted, such as blood clotting, is staggering. Unless you are a hemophiliac, you assume that your blood will clot when you get a minor scratch or cut. You shouldn't. Blood clotting is a complex chemical process. I couldn't believe what I was seeing on a chart which diagrammed the process. Or, what about something everyday like rain? This phenomenon should be so much more simple—warm air rising to its condensation point. Wrong! Scientists vary, disagree and are still not sure what the mechanism is that causes rain.

Scientists were shocked to learn that plants do an accurate mathematical calculation to ensure that they have energy reserves to grow during the night. "They're actually doing maths in a simple, chemical way—that's amazing, it astonished us as scientists to see that," study leader Prof. Alison Smith told BBC News (Helen Briggs, "Plants 'Do Maths' to Control Overnight Food Supplies," BBC News, June 23, 2013, http://www.bbc.com/news/health-22991838). Overnight, when the plant cannot use energy from sunlight to convert carbon dioxide into sugars and starch, it must regulate its starch reserves to ensure they last until dawn. Experiments by scientists at the John Innes Centre in Norwich show that to adjust its starch consumption so precisely, the plant must be performing a mathematical calculation—arithmetic division.

The flight of an insect or bird with whatever nerves, muscles and ability to calculate their flight paths is a marvel to me. A dolphin has a sonar system capability that scientists cannot yet duplicate. A species of locust lays eggs that lie dormant for thirteen years. They finally emerge by the trillions on some kind of cue that is baffling.

How our universe composed of atoms is put together has been the subject of intense research rising to an amazing level of sophistication. The Large Hadron Collider at CERN in Geneva, Switzerland, has brought together scientists from the international physicist community. Wikipedia helps the nonscientist understand what happens. Inside the accelerator, two high-energy particle beams travel at close to the speed of light before they are made to collide. The beams travel in opposite directions in separate beam pipes—two tubes kept at ultrahigh vacuum. They are guided around the accelerator ring by a strong magnetic field. The electromagnets are built from coils of special electric cable that operates in a superconducting state, efficiently conducting electricity without resistance or loss of energy. This requires chilling the magnets to near absolute zero (minus 271.3 degrees Celsius)—a temperature colder than outer space.

I am not implying by using these examples that the Christian life is hopelessly complex to all but the most brilliant theologians. No! We are not to lose sight of our Lord's statement that "unless you are converted and become like children, you will not enter the kingdom of heaven" (Matt. 18:3). He said also, "I praise You, Father . . . that You have hidden these things from the wise and intelligent and have revealed them to infants" (Matt. 11:25). Where is the balance? What do we need to know? We are to understand what we should if we are to be mature—to grow up. The writer of Hebrews says, "Leaving the elementary teaching about the Christ, let us press on to maturity" (Heb. 6:1).

The *purpose of* our journey is to step back and look at the Christian life from a higher vantage point than we normally do—like the mature people of whom the writer of Hebrews speaks. As plants do their math, we are to do our work too. We are involved in a great number of growth areas during the course of our Christian life. We live through various stages.

The apostle John speaks of children, young people and fathers (1 John 2:12–14). We have tasks in each one of these stages. One may be called on to be obedient by faith when she is down, instead of giving in to irresponsible behavior like she did in the past. For another, it's the focus of abiding in Christ (staying in relationship with Him) throughout a day or week and finding out how this state is to be achieved. Someone else is attempting to learn how "to pray without ceasing." Another is developing the habit of meditating on one verse of the Bible for each day of her work week. Jim is prospering as an executive in a large company and is making a mid–six figure salary. He is trying to figure out what his financial stewardship should be.

Complexity

So then, let's step back and look at the components of change, development and growth for a life shaped, formed and matured in the course of life. Our purpose is not to include every element that makes up the growth package for Christian living. Rather, we will attempt to expand our field of vision so that we live a more complete life and find a path to greater maturity. *Long-term change in a quick-fix world* is the umbrella title we are placing over our study.

We have only the slightest understanding of what was involved in the Incarnation. Becoming like Jesus who became like us is comprehended fully in the mind of God and only partially in ours. It is our task to grow as fully as is possible for each of us. It is an amazingly good, important and worthwhile task. Taking a look at how long-term change occurs over the course of life is our adventure and task.

A final note: I like cinnamon rolls with lots of icing. I bought some today that were loaded with it. They weigh a quarter pound apiece and each one contains eleven grams of saturated fat—not good! I counted forty-eight ingredients.

Buy a Cinnabon Classic cinnamon roll in a local mall, go to your local bakery, or buy some at a grocery store and two things will be true. They will each have different ingredients but all of them will taste like a cinnamon roll. No two authors treat the ingredients of the Christian life exactly alike. None of the seven hundred books I saw on the shelves of a Christian college and the three hundred in our Christian bookstore did either. However, like the rolls bought at various places, they all taste like cinnamon rolls. We are majoring on an overview of the Christian life in which we highlight elements that lead to real maturity, life formation and a final stamp, "approved." We will find this spectacular panorama painted with broad brush strokes across the landscape of the Bible. And may you be blessed in reading this or any other book on the Christian life which is true to the Bible and the faith which was once delivered to the saints (Jude 3).

For Reflection and Discussion

1. Have you found the Christian life to be more complex than you anticipated or has it been a matter of managing a few basics well?
2. Have you found your Christian experience to be more confusing, tangled, or unmanageable than you anticipated?
3. Would you feel comfortable writing a basic manual on living the Christian life for new believers?
4. What are your practices that keep you grounded as a follower of Christ?

3

Long-Term Change

Barriers and Roadblocks

A few Christian business owners had come together for a retreat. Long-term change was the theme and here is a question I shot at all of us: "What has prevented or delayed the process you have wanted in selected areas of your life?" We would all come up with our list if asked the question, "What factors make long-term change difficult or unlikely?"

For our purposes, I select only a few factors related to why we generally fall short of our potential in fully growing up as Christians. I do so to illustrate why we need to look at the big picture. In the sports world, gimmicks work for only so long. Using a flea flicker in which a running back tosses the ball back to the quarterback for a long pass works for a couple of times perhaps. These plays can't substitute for a well-rounded offense in which blocking, pass protection or passing routes are run well. Likewise, we are looking for a balanced Christian life.

A fragment of something I read has stayed with me. It is the idea that the enormity of our ego really works against us in our pursuit of the will of God. We hang on to health, finances, family, career, goals, retirement, status, security, personal pride and other aspects of our lives so that it is difficult to keep God's will enshrined above them all. Our own self-interest, self-absorption or egocentricity work against long-term change.

We sell out so cheaply! A lonely man with a spouse and family sells out for an evening of pleasure when he is on the road. A young woman sells out her life to marry a man who has money and status and charm but lacks every other asset to be a good husband and father. When we have felt insecure, most of us have sacrificed what we shouldn't to gain acceptance with people who were unnecessary or debilitating to our lives. I find it heartbreaking to watch people sell out so cheaply, and frightening to see the same tendencies in me!

Addictions, deeply rooted disturbances in our emotions or personalities, dysfunctional habit patterns, or failed coping strategies reinforced by hundreds of repetitions are not easily eliminated. A revolting pattern of sin, an embarrassing distortion in our lives, or destructive practices that have been with us for years don't disappear easily. We may have prayed, fasted, read self-help books, received counseling and confessed our faults to others while asking for their support—and all without changing.

How can we experience change in these troubling areas of our lives that cause shame and damage to us and those we love? The apostle Paul's lament is, "I am doing the very thing I do not want . . . a prisoner of the law of sin. . . . Who will set me free from the body of this death?" (Rom. 7:20, 23–24). Doing what we don't want to do—being prisoners when we should be free, crying out to be released from what is killing us when we should be flourishing—so often describes our sad experience.

Another one that nibbles away and causes us to dissipate our lives is the distraction that we endure on so many fronts. How many times have you seen people eating together and all are focused on their cell phones? Go to a film and count the lighted screens of mobile devices as people send a final text or check messages.

During a conversation, one of our granddaughters suddenly went to her cell phone. She wasn't tuning out on us—just checking the Internet to get information on the topic we were discussing. Today, we have potential which was impossible to imagine a century ago. We can have the world in the palm of our hands.

For many of us, television eats away at the time we could spend in much higher priority activities. It is no wonder that people who are really serious about their life development as sojourners with God unplug their TVs for a while.

We have indicated only some of the barriers to finding long-term change or a life well developed with God in the few years we have to do so. You would have your own list of the odds against long-term change.

Well-known Christians who should demonstrate the highest standards of Christian living all too frequently fall. They testify as well that the odds of successful long-term change are against us. A current situation involves a Christian leader who has hosted perhaps a couple of million earnest Christians for his seminars. Many keep his thick notebooks filled with excellent materials for Christian living. And yet he faced accusations of inappropriate behavior toward young women employed in his organization.

If things like this happen to highly respected Christian leaders, what hope is there for people like us who fall in the category of ordinary Christians? We are looking for a more complete picture that will better our odds!

For Reflection and Discussion
1. Why is it so hard to live the kind of Christian life you desire?
2. What things contribute to your failures?
3. What is your strategy to experience the growth you are striving for as a Christian?
4. Do you have good role models for your life as a godly person? Are they an encouragement and help to stay the course in your life?

4

Long-Term Change

Culmination

Sometimes, starting at the end helps us find the path to get there. A high school coach may tell his football team at the first August practice, "This season is all about one thing—getting to the state championships!" One of our granddaughters played college soccer and a motivational theme was selected to start the season's competition. One year a poster for the team pictured them on a tarmac in front of an airplane which could carry the whole team. The symbolism is obvious. "Let's get on the plane together and fly to a national championship." They won three out of four national championships while she was there. Starting at the end can lead to a powerful focus in which we integrate everything into a single focus. It helps to put everything together.

We too are starting at the end while we are still at the beginning in our focused study. Romans 8:29 gives us the end result of long-term change. "For those whom He foreknew, He also predestined to become conformed to the image of His Son, so that He would be the firstborn among many brethren."

Incredible is not too strong a word here. The *incredible* culmination of long-term change is *that He would be the firstborn among many brethren.* Heaven, eternity and the afterlife are to be populated with those who are His brothers and sisters—those who have become like Him. *Conformed to His image* is the idea used in this verse. Ephesians 4:13, 15 reinforces this astonishing idea: "Until we all attain to the unity of the faith, and of the knowledge of the Son of God, to a mature man, to the measure of the stature which belongs to the fullness of Christ . . . we are to grow up in all aspects unto Him who is the head, even Christ."

I was talking with a person who owns a successful, high profile business that operates internationally. Here was my question to him, "In the eternal state, will your business be included in the scenario we have in Romans 8:29?" His answer of course was, "No!" I didn't need to tell him, but I did anyway, "*You* will be His treasure, not your business—it is dispensable."

What about the great buildings, museums, castles, palaces, government buildings, libraries, art works, or global businesses that span the world? Some of these will make it beyond time and space, won't they? Again, the answer is negative. There is no indication that God will take much of anything out of this present age but US!

The prize God will transfer to the eternal state is that group of people who have become like Christ, conformed to His image, His sisters and brothers in the truest and deepest sense. A striking image occurs in Hebrews 12:23, "The spirits of the righteous made perfect." Perfected in the essence of our beings is the idea. Growing long-term and developing as followers of Christ over the course of our lives is our task, and our Hebrews verse assures us that it will eventually be complete.

Long-Term Change: Culmination

God is working with us now toward what will be perfect then! What is going to happen in the future is occurring now incrementally. As we grow and develop, the now will transition to a perfected future.

This process is particularly linked to the work of the Holy Spirit as the following critical verses indicate: "We serve in newness of the Spirit. . . . For the law of the Spirit of life in Christ Jesus has set you free from the law of sin and of death . . . so that the requirement of the Law might be fulfilled in us, who do not walk according to the flesh but according to the Spirit. . . . We all, . . . beholding as in a mirror the glory of the Lord, are being transformed into the same image from glory to glory, just as from the Lord, the Spirit" (Rom. 7:6; 8:2, 4; 2 Cor. 3:18; see chap. 8, "The Ministry of the Holy Spirit").

We have footnoted the end result of long-term change. Becoming like Christ, taking on His image, being conformed to what He is like at the deepest levels of our being, gaining the fullest stature of which we are capable in what is most important—that's the idea. This is where long-term change is leading us. How long does it take? The obvious answer is a lifetime! And it will still be a work in progress when we finally finish our respective life stages.

This journey could be described in many ways: *long*, demanding, multifaceted, incredibly important, complex, often convoluted, many ups and downs, bitter failures and shining successes, sometimes confusing or desperate, incredibly painful, deeply fulfilling, ranging from hopeless to hopeful, or demanding beyond everything we might have imagined.

Long-term change is distinctive or unique to each of us but the same in essence. No one will read this book at exactly the same stage, intensity or with the same set of needs. However, we are heading toward that state when "we all attain to the unity of the faith . . . to a mature man, to the measure of the stature which belongs to the fullness of Christ" (Eph. 4:13).

Romans 8:29 gives us the goal. In the sports world, it's like the coach. "Men, this season is about one thing—getting to the state championships." In the same way, we are focusing on being and becoming intimate associates of Christ.

For Reflection and Discussion

1. Does it help prepare you for what is to come to begin where the process of the long-term change will end?
2. Could you comment on how important or motivating it is for you that you will eventually be so much like Christ that you will be like His closest relative?
3. Do you feel strongly that you are truly on the way to this future spoken of in Romans 8:29?
4. If you are living toward this end, how does it help you exclude what is extraneous now?

Part 2

Long-Term Change

We Are Not Alone

When you think of growing as a Christian, developing sorely needed disciplines or overcoming habits or sins that plague you, I think I can read your mind. You think of what you need to do, the effort you need to expend and how you should shape up or get your act together. You no doubt pray, "Lord help me!" but you feel the burden to make it happen and overcome your weaknesses.

Our good intentions are admirable and so is our hunger to know God better and improve our walk with Him. However, we are not alone. In the Upper Room Discourse, the Lord promised that He would not leave us to struggle along in a solitary, lonely battle. "I will not leave you as orphans; I will come to you" (John 14:18).

After my conversion just following high school, I was anchored by a few verses while I fought battles which I often lost. One verse which shone in my dark moments was 2 Corinthians 2:14: "But thanks be to God, who always leads us in triumph in Christ."

A deep confidence formed that "I'm going to win even though I am falling down, getting up and repeating the whole process all over again. I'm not doing very well, but the Lord will see to it that I win." This verse seems to be rooted in the analogy of a great Roman general who returns with a large procession of those who are part of his victory celebration. "It's not just about me. It's about being part of something much broader, bigger and more significant than whether I'm a very average Christian the rest of my life. I will be victorious because of what I am part of—the triumph of Christ. It doesn't all depend on me."

Philippians 1:6 took me further—so much so that I memorized it many years ago. "Being confident of this very thing, that he which hath begun a good work in you will perform it until the day of Jesus Christ" (KJV). It was simple. Who began the good work in me? Who was going to finish it? The Lord!

Philippians 2:12–13 harmonizes the relationship between what I am supposed to do and what God promises to perform. The counterbalance of these two verses introduces the section to follow and sets the balance for the rest of the book. "Work out your salvation with fear and trembling; for it is God who is at work in you, both to will and to work for His good pleasure."

The reason these verses set the tone for the rest of the book is obvious. We are to work on long-term change because God is working too. Our salvation in Christ is magnificent beyond our ability to know fully. We are to work it out the rest of our lives while He is helping to give us a will to do so and working on our behalf as well so that the process actually happens.

5

The New Birth

My original title for this chapter was, "Do We Have a Baby Here? The New Birth into a Family." Chuck Colson's 1976 best seller, *Born Again*, catapulted *being born again* into the national spotlight, but the phrase soon became trivialized or laughed at. How might we answer the cynical question, "Why in the world do I need to be *born again?*"

There is no such thing as a California condor with a ten-foot wingspan riding the updrafts over the Grand Canyon who did not begin his journey as a helpless hatchling. You won't find a 350-pound lineman who was not first expelled from his mother's womb. A skyscraper would never have happened without someone throwing the first shovel of dirt. As an ancient Chinese philosopher said, "A journey of a thousand miles begins with a single step" (*The Way of Lao-Tzu*).

Living and maturing in the Christian life is a lifetime process. It is multifaceted, multidimensional and involves too many variables to allow a simple formula. However, the new birth is the starting point or nonnegotiable beginning for our lifelong trip. Whether we come from a religious or nonreligious background, are Coptic or Orthodox, have a Muslim or Jewish upbringing, a bishop in the Roman Catholic Church or the churchgoer in a small independent church, a young mom in a cramped apartment in Beijing or her counterpart in the Amazon basin, a CEO of a multinational company or the guy who scrubs the toilets there after hours—like Nicodemus in John 3 we all begin from the same starting point.

Romans 3 drives home the point relentlessly that we are *all* estranged from God. We can't be fixed up, patched up, touched up or uploaded by our own efforts. This terrible news becomes wonderful news when the Lord Jesus Christ provides a new birth that exceeds what we might do for ourselves in the best of all the worlds. What He does for us must be received freely. It can't be earned, augmented or improved—just received!

The *new birth* teaching in John's Gospel is underscored like a quarterback's double pump before he passes the football. He gets the attention of his opponents and everybody else in the stadium. Jesus prefaces His pronouncement about the new birth with "verily, verily," or "truly, truly" in our modern versions. It's like saying, "I couldn't emphasize more what I am about to say."

He addressed His words to Nicodemus, who was mature, influential and had an established platform in life. He was a *ruler of the Jews.* His integrity or sincerity was not questioned by the Lord. It just wasn't enough. A physical birth followed by a spiritual birth was given to him as a *sine qua non* (Latin: without which there is nothing).

His night interview with Jesus was transformational, changing the course of his life. Nicodemus later put everything on the line when he came alongside of Joseph of Arimathea to play a role in the way the body of the Lord was handled. This type of radical change is not uncommon when a person is *born again.*

There are no shortcuts. According to the apostle Paul, in Romans 4, this is where both Abraham and David started centuries before Nicodemus's night interview. When they took God at His word as did Nicodemus, they got their start with God. They could pass "Go."

There are no shortcuts. Paul's language is pointed and unambiguous in Ephesians 2:8–9: "For by grace you have been saved through faith; and that not of yourselves, it is the gift of God; not as a result of works, so that no one may boast." The new birth can come about only by faith. It can't originate or be generated from the individual. It is a gift from God and is never produced by self-effort. Thus, no one can ever boast.

Our lifetime journey of long-term change must begin with being born again into God's family. And when we are born again, we are not alone. We become part of a family. The New Testament references this so often. First Corinthians 12:13 speaks of being baptized into one body—that is, being made an organic part of the body of Christ, the church. The spiritual gifts outlined in Romans 12 and 1 Corinthians 12 are given to the body of which each of us is a part. A section of 1 Corinthians claims that this family is so exclusive that we shouldn't even go to court against a brother or sister.

Paul calls on two members of the family in the church at Philippi—Euodia and Syntyche—to reestablish their relationship. He calls on other members of this spiritual household to stand alongside them as well.

All the apostle Paul's church epistles are written to spiritual families in various communities. Likewise, the apostle John addresses the seven churches in Turkey (Revelation 2–3) as integral and separated bodies of believers.

It all makes sense. A baby is born and integrated into a family. My heart is warmed as I see two, three, or even four generations of family together in obviously bonded relationships. There is nothing like it. Putting it in Christian terms, this spiritual-family relationship idea is brought together in Ephesians 3:14–15: "I bow my knees before the Father, from whom every family in heaven and on earth derives its name." When an individual is *new birthed*, she or he is never alone. The new birth brings us into the family of God, and long-term change as a follower of Christ begins there too. When is the last time you breathed a prayer of thanks for being *born again*?

For Reflection and Discussion
1. Why is it important to be clear about what the new birth provides and how it takes place?
2. Are you assured that you are born again? What might you do if you are not?
3. How passionate are you about helping others to be born again into God's family?
4. Do you know how to share this message in a variety of contexts with different kinds of people?

6

God's Master Plan

Did you follow your parents' plan for your life? Cain and Esau certainly didn't, as the early chapters of Genesis note. Thirteenth-century Saint Francis of Assisi was disowned by his wealthy silk merchant father when he chose to follow God in a life of poverty. The issue in this chapter is not whether we are following our parents' wishes but whether we are following God's. Had Saint Francis followed his father's plan, one of the great saints of the church would have been lost to us.

As believers, we understand that God has some kind of plan for our lives. We cannot take a big view of the Christian life without being aware of it. Here, we take note of how this plan is critical in the long process of growing up.

We have referenced Philippians 1:6 and 2:12–13 previously. These verses inform us that God's plan is decreed over the course of our lives. He is involved in initiating our journey and is the Stakeholder in seeing it through to its culmination over the course of our lives. While we are required to work on developing our lives with God, we know that He is also working.

"How well is the plan working out in my life?" is a persistent question for some of us. John 15:16, one of the great verses in the Gospels, speaks to us about the plan and our relation to it: "You did not choose Me but I chose you, and appointed you that you would go and bear fruit, and that your fruit would remain, so that whatever you ask of the Father in My name He may give to you."

This verse is powerful and pointed. The message includes the following: (1) We are the recipients of His choice. We made the team! (2) We have a divine appointment to produce fruit. What is this fruit? For a start, it refers to godly character and a righteous life that God produces in and through us by His Spirit. From such a life in Christ come good works, deeds done as acts of loving one's neighbor as oneself for the love of God, for example. A predetermined plan for our lives involves a productivity that is permanent. This means that we will not live in such a way that we leave nothing behind of value when we die. (3) The plan calls for us to be engaged in praying or seeking what is involved in this course of action which lies ahead of us.

We appreciate leaders who exercise authority in all the best ways. This verse emphasizes that we are chosen by the Lord Himself. A plan comes with His choosing. It involves living a valuable life with results that last beyond it and with resources to make it happen. God has a time/space plan. Jesus chooses us to operate that plan. It is a bigger plan than any one of us can fully comprehend individually. We will see elsewhere that God works to make sure we are aligned with it. We are urged in John 15:16 to cash in on the plan and ask for everything needed to make it a reality.

Ephesians 2:10 adds another touch: "For we are His workmanship, created in Christ Jesus for good works, which God prepared beforehand so that we would walk in them." Note first that we are chosen or selected to be masterpieces. The Greek gives the idea of master craftsmanship. Second Corinthians 5:17 speaks of us as *new*—newly minted, if you will. This status necessarily involves both what we become and what we produce as highly privileged people.

A purpose idea which follows in Ephesians 2:10 indicates as well that we are to accomplish divinely ordered and prepared tasks which empower God's plan in the world. Note three of the ideas packed into this verse: (1) We are "created in Christ Jesus for good works." Enough said, is a logical response here. We are purposed to produce something in God's master plan. (2) "Prepared beforehand" is the next idea. This statement presupposes that God is omniscient, knowing the end from the beginning. His plan was established before we were grafted into it. (3) "That we would walk in them" places responsibility on us. Whatever translation you are using for this verse, the idea remains that we have some kind of choice in the matter. We are not robots. We are not programmed. We must cooperate.

God is involved in our long-term development and we are too. It is like a divinely orchestrated dance in which we strenuously attempt to keep step with our Partner. We are called on to participate in a sovereignly established plan that gets very specific.

Long-term change involves a lifetime of our own effort. An entire section of the book is devoted to what is required in this process. However, we have begun with the divine side of the total picture. We are included in the plan that calls for us to play a critical role in what God has chosen to work out in the world. He takes responsibility to call us and make us masterpieces of His making so that it happens. We are called on to cooperate!

For Reflection and Discussion
1. To what extent are you aware and desirous of cooperating with the divine plan as it applies to you?
2. Do you have a pretty good grasp of what this plan is all about in your case? Or is your understanding murky?
3. Are you confident that *the plan* we have explored applies to you?
4. Are you generally at peace that you are cooperating with *this plan*?

7

The Bible

Last night was Halloween. Suppose one of the children on this wet night went home with a pillowcase full of candy. Her parents exclaimed excitedly that this would be her breakfast and lunch on school days for the next few weeks. Before school, she would just need to grab a Payday, Snickers, or Skittles as she went out the door. "Inconceivable!" you say.

Sadly enough, it is not uncommon for Christians to have no Bible in their diet for an entire work week. Before looking at its *use*, we need to consider the *place* of the Bible.

There are reasons why an elementary school child should not be limited to a diet of candy and powerful factors why a believer needs the Bible in his or her daily diet. We select a few. In John 17:17, Scripture is spoken of as the agent by which we are sanctified or separated to a life with and for God. The Bible is powerful or sufficient, if used often and well, to place a boundary around us to set us apart to a life worth living—a sanctified life. Psalm 119:104 speaks of it as a radar system that helps us spot and avoid what is false. Without the Bible, we can be vulnerable to floating along with the rest of humanity toward anything but a good end.

The great manifesto in 2 Timothy 3:16–17 gives us the unique and unparalleled *place* of the Bible. It is the only book in the world and history of mankind that is inspired or God-breathed. It is our *textbook*. "All Scripture is inspired by God and profitable for teaching, for reproof, for correction, for training in righteousness; so that the man of God may be adequate, equipped for every good work."

What the Bible does for us is better than a high school, college, or graduate degree. These degrees, valuable as they are, may or may not equip a person for life or make a certain career a sure thing. The promise here is that the Bible prepares us for true success in life in terms of character and conduct. This equips us to pursue the good and the excellent in whatever we do in our careers or occupations. The truth and wisdom of God's Word can protect us from the trap of striking success and spectacular failure all rolled up in one life.

Young people are singled out in Psalm 119:9. Through the Scriptures a young person can be kept from a polluted life. Could this be even more important now than when these words were written almost three thousand years ago? Today opportunities, attractions and perverted practices for young people are present in many forms. The Bible directs them to a clean life as an excellent preparation for the rest of life.

I am saddened at how little wealth is able to make people happy. Time after time, the claim is made in the Bible that it is a resource, treasure or asset beyond any wealth, fortune, or accumulated possession we can gain. Psalm 19:10 places Scripture above fourteen-karat gold. Psalm 119, the longest chapter in the Bible, is a lavish celebration of the available riches of the Bible.

The few references we have noted regarding the *place* of the Bible in the life of a Christian are sufficient to steer us away from a diet of spiritual junk food when a fabulous diet is readily available. Let's get up and into the Word every day—even in pajamas is okay!

The psalmist had a great analogy for expressing the *place* the Word of God occupied in his life. "Your statutes are my songs in the house of my pilgrimage" (Ps. 119:54). There are a lot of songs we can sing in our pilgrimage, but none of them can equal the *place* of the revealed Word for us. In subsequent chapters we focus on *using* the Bible. We will look at how important it is for us to make biblical promises ours personally. The timeless practice of meditation will be demonstrated as being critical for us today even though we are long past the time when memory was a foundational mode of learning and historical preservation.

For Reflection and Discussion

1. Are you treasuring the Bible for your own life versus a general appreciation of it for everyone?
2. Comment on your own journey with the Bible.
3. How would you describe the *place* it occupies with you?
4. Are you comfortable calling others to recognize and act on its importance for them?

8

The Ministry of the Holy Spirit

A more mature and older Christian couple took me under their wing when I was an undergraduate at the University of Illinois. They were charismatic and dynamic Christians. They prayed that I might experience the same ministry of the Holy Spirit they did.

When I returned home, I was speechless at what I saw on the vacant property between our home and the local golf course. It required two semis to bring in the tent and equipment for the charismatic revival taking place a few steps from our home. I said, "So, Lord, this is what you are doing to answer Jim and Cathy's prayer—bringing a big charismatic tent revival right to my backyard."

Obviously, I had to attend a service. I did so and heard a message which emphasized the gift of tongues. It didn't work. I didn't receive the gift and never have. I have searched Old and New Testaments on the Holy Spirit, have stood in awe and utter silence over His ministry, and consult amazing verses on

His provision almost every week, and they burn with an aura of glory each time. But I don't have the gift of tongues that Jim and Cathy wanted for me.

In this chapter, we are bypassing such issues to focus on aspects of the Holy Spirit's ministry that are generally accepted by the great majority of Christians. This book does not allow us the opportunity for a detailed study of pneumatology—the doctrine of the Holy Spirit. We merely highlight primary facets of His ministry to believers today. The Holy Spirit is an essential, irreplaceable Person in the life and long-term change process of the believer.

First: *Giver of new birth.* Our Lord emphasizes in John 3:5–6 that the Holy Spirit is inextricably a part of the new-birth process. If you are a *born again* Christian, the Spirit of God was involved when you became a member of God's family. Without this genesis or beginning in our lives, we lack a foundation on which to build long-term change. If we cannot extricate the Holy Spirit from genuine conversion, neither can we remove Him from the authentic changes we desire.

Second: *Life source.* John's Gospel is a rich source of revelation about what the Holy Spirit does on behalf of believers. What is given to us in John 7:37–39 is striking. Our Lord notes that the Holy Spirit will be like a spring of life-giving water that cannot be contained within us but will overflow to others. This is an awe-inspiring claim. When our lives have been dry and arid, we have the privilege of being so filled with life as God intended it that we can't contain it.

Third: *Presence.* A truth about the Holy Spirit which assures us is revealed further in our Lord's Upper Room Discourse. He is our divine permanent Presence. In this role, He is our Helper. We do not function without His aid. This promise is recorded in John 14:16–17: "I will ask the Father, and He will give you another Helper, that He may be with you forever; that is the Spirit of truth, whom the world cannot receive, because it does not see Him or know Him, *but* you know Him because He abides with you and will be in you." He adds the statement we have previously noted, "I will not leave you as orphans; I will come to you" (John 14:18). We are not alone or unsupported in the long-term change process.

Fourth: *Teacher.* The knowledge of Christ is transforming. We wish we could have time with our Lord as did His disciples during the three and one-half years recorded in the Gospels. "Perhaps I would be a better follower and be more confident that I really know Him if I would have had that experience," we may say to ourselves. Jesus gives us the assurance we need in His discourse recorded in John 13–17.

We can and do know our Lord in genuine fashion as a result of the Holy Spirit's intimate ministry to us. The message given directly by our Lord needs no further comment. "But when He, the Spirit of truth, comes, He will guide you into all the truth; for He will not speak on His own initiative, but whatever He hears, He will speak; and He will disclose to you what is to come. He will glorify Me, for He will take of Mine and will disclose *it* to you" (John 16:13–14).

The Holy Spirit becomes our divine Teacher and helps us know the Lord as if we were present during His earthly life. In fact the disciples were not *A students* until they too had received the ministry of the Holy Spirit, as recorded in Acts. The apostle John emphasizes this truth again in 1 John 2:27. "The anointing which you received from Him abides in you, and you have no need for anyone to teach you; but as His anointing teaches you about all things, and is true and is not a lie, and just as it has taught you, you abide in Him."

Fifth: *Law of life.* Paul writes about the sad fact that believers, in spite of being declared righteous through Christ, are still prone and even prisoners to sin. "I am not practicing what I would like to do, but I am doing the very thing I hate" (Rom. 7:15). But in the next chapter, he teaches emphatically what is also taught elsewhere in the New Testament: The Holy Spirit is the divine inner presence who is the *law of life* to free us from the sin we can't shake, even after the new birth. This is a great study and an even better fact! "For the law of the Spirit of life in Christ Jesus has set you free from the law of sin and death" (Rom. 8:2). The apostle gives the idea again in Galatians 5:16, "Walk by the Spirit, and you will not carry out the desire of the flesh."

Sixth: *Leader.* Who of us has not felt a pressing need for guidance, direction or wisdom for life-changing decisions? Romans 8, a pinnacle chapter on the ministry of Holy Spirit, includes His guiding or leading ministry. "For all who are being led by the Spirit of God, these are sons of God" (Rom. 8:14).

In this verse, being led by Him is set forth as an inescapable reality and requirement. If we do not experience this interactive relationship with the Holy Spirit in which He guides us, the validity of our relationship to God could be called into question.

A shoe leather example of this guidance is recorded in Acts 16:6. "They passed through the Phrygian and Galatian region, having been forbidden by the Holy Spirit to speak the word in Asia." The Holy Spirit directed the movements of Paul and his associates. He directed what they did and where they traveled and, we might assume, their strategy. The Macedonian call was no doubt authored by the Holy Spirit. It is not surprising that He dictated the course correction that led to the establishment of the first church in Europe. They were commanded to go from Asia Minor toward Europe after what we label as the Macedonian call.

Seventh: *Producer of character.* *Create* is perhaps not the best word to describe what happens when a fruit tree ends up with a crop of wonderful fruit on it. I think *produce* is the best word. The ingredients are all present in the fruit tree. The process just has to happen.

Likewise, when we become members of God's family with all the ingredients that are provided for us, this amazing *fruit* process can also occur in us. What is beautiful, striking and godlike can be present in us to the glory of God and sometimes to the wonderment of those who observe Christians who are filled with the *fruit of the Spirit.*

In cooperation with the believer, the Holy Spirit produces fruit—whatever in our lives pleases or is valuable to God. It is precisely like the fruit tree which produces something that is valuable for human consumption.

In the context of our study, the *fruit of the Spirit* is critical to our long-term change and development. This process and the product formed over a lifetime *will not* happen without the Holy Spirit's participation. Galatians 5:22–23 is the familiar passage which states this essential truth: "But the fruit of the Spirit is love, joy, peace, patience, kindness, goodness, faithfulness, gentleness, self-control; against such things there is no law."

Eighth: *Creative deliverer.* Paul paid a heavy price for his ministry in Philippi, but it resulted in the first church in Europe. It also involved a cruel beating and being jailed. This painful course of his life continued. He was under house arrest in Rome.

There was more! Prayer on his behalf buoyed him up. There was more yet! The ministry of the Holy Spirit would bring about *creative deliverance*. As Paul says in Philippians 1:19, "I know that this will turn out for my deliverance through your prayers and the provision of the Spirit of Jesus Christ."

That is, what was distasteful, difficult and undesirable for the apostle was to be transformed into a life-changing experience. It's the old story. God is able to take the worst and make it, if not the best, wonderful in the eventual result. He claims that the Author of this process is the Holy Spirit.

The application to our lives and the ongoing change in them is obvious. All of us have jail-type, constricting, dangerous and falling-in-the-mud experiences we would never choose. But through the prayers of God's people and the ministry of the Holy Spirit in *creative deliverance*, these ugly circumstances can be changed. They can be transformed into that which is critical in the formation and development of our lives, as we become who and what we can be!

Ninth: *Giver of gifts.* The Holy Spirit gives the gifts that are required for the full functioning of the body of Christ—the church. First Corinthians 12:4, 7 states that there are "varieties of gifts, but the same Spirit. . . . To each one is given the manifestation of the Spirit for the common good." He lists the gifts specifying that they come from the Spirit. The next chapter on the church highlights this phenomenon.

A final note becomes a warning. The ministry of the Holy Spirit cannot be taken carelessly or lightly. We are commanded not to "quench the Spirit" (1 Thess. 5:19). Peter claimed that Ananias and Sapphira lied to the Holy Spirit (Acts 5) and it cost them their lives. Jesus said that blasphemy against the Holy Spirit would not be forgiven (Matt. 12:31–32). We could say,

"Christian, be blessed by the ministry of the Holy Spirit but beware of being careless." If we are ever to go the distance and be changed all the way to the depth of our being, the Holy Spirit must be involved.

For Reflection and Discussion

1. How aware of or responsive to the ministry of the Holy Spirit have you been?
2. Why might devoting some additional time to study, reflect, or pray over His ministry strengthen your life with God?
3. From the nine ministries of the Holy Spirit we selected, which are the most important to you?
4. How might you speak of the ministry of the Holy Spirit to a new Christian?

9

Long-Term Change Together

The Church

We are sometimes conflicted about our relationship to the Church. How many complaints have you heard? Has anyone said in your hearing, "The church is only interested in my money"? Have you ever thought, "If I was doing it, I would use angels instead of humans. People always mess things up"? As years pass and my experiences in the church pile up, I am convinced that there is no easy way to do church!

The apostle Paul's church epistles underscore my conclusion. Take 1 Corinthians, for example—the first epistle to this church. People were getting drunk at the Lord's Table. Church members who had money ate abundantly during this sacred time, while poor brothers and sisters didn't have anything. A situation involving incest existed! Christians were fighting over whether Paul or someone else was superior.

If this was the best a church directly related to an apostle could do, what about ours today? I once helped a local church select elders. I was told that a fist fight broke out previously when its leaders attempted to address this issue. Is there much hope for churches today that are two thousand years removed from the New Testament? Paul said, "I know that after my departure savage wolves will come in among you, not sparing the flock; and from among your own selves men will arise, speaking perverse things, to draw away the disciples after them" (Acts 20:29–30). They have had a long time to do their dirty work in the church and have been successful down the centuries.

Someone has said that evangelicals love the gospel but dislike the church. But the fact remains that the church—universally and in its local forms and as broken as it might be—is critical to our lives. If you are a Christian, you are part of the church even though you may never darken the door of one. First Corinthians 12:13 says, "For by one Spirit we were all baptized into one body, whether Jews or Greeks, whether slaves or free, and we were all made to drink of one Spirit." The idea is that the Holy Spirit makes each person who has become a child of God through faith in Christ an organic part of the church—the body of Christ.

So then, we are not alone. *We are supposed to experience long-term change together!* There have always been lone-ranger types in God's family. Elijah and Elisha appear to come out of nowhere for their prophetic ministries among God's people. Saint Patrick arrived in Ireland like a king without a court, after having been a slave for six years there as a young man. The apostle Paul went alone to the Arabian Peninsula for his early spiritual formation but lived and served as an apostle in a fabric of relationships.

The norm is spiritual community. Leaders who violate this principle often pay an ugly price. I remember a high profile leader who would appear on TV with supporting scholars waiting in the background. He was like a king surrounded and separate from his court. I would have liked to ask him two questions: "To whom are you accountable? Who has the right to ask you the hard questions?"

Sometime after I saw him on TV, headlines announced his arrest after he propositioned a woman. Another national leader responsible for many thousands of Christians from various denominations was brought down when a homosexual scandal caught up with him. Did either of these men have spiritual peers who had access to the recesses of their lives? Christian superstars without support or accountability are in danger. And so are we all.

When the Life Serve project was launched, one of these hard questions came my way. "Charles, are you doing this because you can't work with anyone else?" My answer was, "This is a right question to ask!" I had the benefit of being older and recognizing the cost of heading down a blind alley. The hardnosed question was worth temporary discomfort. It was an insurance policy!

Maintain relationships. Strong relationships are assumed and are the norm in the New Testament. A powerful recent book on ministry in the Muslim world observes that independent type Christians who are not ready to be part of a spiritual community are not only a stumbling block to the non-Christians they are trying to reach but leave themselves open to even more dangerous vulnerability in the Muslim world. Whatever the country or culture, healthy relationships must be maintained even when they become strained.

As mentioned earlier, the apostle Paul addressed a dangerous relational issue with two women in the church at Philippi. They are famous because they demonstrate the principle that we can be helped in maintaining the relationships required in which we grow, serve and fulfill our life mission. Thanks to Euodia and Syntyche for being object lessons! They were surrounded by those who could protect them, but who would also suffer loss if they went their separate ways.

Here is what the apostle had to say to them in the context of their close-knit church body in Philippi: "I urge Euodia and I urge Syntyche to live in harmony in the Lord. Indeed, true companion, I ask you also to help these women who have shared my struggle in the cause of the gospel, together with Clement also and the rest of my fellow workers" (Phil. 4:2–3).

Why was the relationship of the two women so important anyway? My answer became clearer when we visited the ruins of Philippi. I knelt by the stream side where Lydia and her friends were evangelized by the apostle Paul. Why? This was first time the gospel had moved beyond Asia to Europe—the initial planting of the church in Europe! You and I were there in Philippi! The gospel movement westward eventually made it all the way to North America and beyond so that we were included!

The Philippian church was seminal. What happened there could affect the many thousands of churches that would follow when the boundary was breached and the gospel would move to the ends of the earth.

We could push our point further. Paul and Silas paid a terrible price for the establishment of the Philippian church. You may recall the Acts account which records their savage beating after preaching. They were thrown into jail and put into stocks so that there was no way to treat their wounds or reduce their pain.

It was an insult to this historical saga and the almost transcendent beginning in Philippi for two church members to be bickering or fighting. Couldn't we easily make a case about the regrettable situations today in which fellow church members are at each other's throats? We insult basic truths and realities when we can't get along in our local churches. Unlike Philippi, today churches frequently lack the resources, procedures or means to deal with relational breakdowns. We often steer away from mediating conflicts or (only as a last resort) stepping into situations that demand church discipline. Being a community that functions fully is so difficult in our current culture in which we tend to live separate, independent lives. Does your church have a means of helping its members sort out troubled relationships? Paul asked for help in a delicate situation so that these two women might be able to live *in harmony in the Lord.* He gives us a gold standard for working through conflicts that pop up so often in church fellowships.

Today, difficult situations that would keep us from growing together are often handled by a counselor or therapist. Pastoral counseling by someone on the church staff is available in some churches. Small groups account for a great deal of care in these and other situations. The bottom line is that we are to grow together; if we are to do so, relationships must be maintained.

Benefits from our combined abilities. One of the reasons the powerful fabric of relationships is so important is that we share divinely given capabilities. These varied abilities are called spiritual gifts, and they are irreplaceable for our long-term growth, which is facilitated by the special abilities of others.

The apostle Paul specifies these in Romans 12:6–8 and 1 Corinthians 12:7–11. They include the ability to teach so that we are equipped with what we need to know to grow. A special ability called the gift of mercy means that we can extend compassion when a member of the community or outside it is vulnerable and needy. Further, special enhanced abilities to serve, exhort, give, lead, give wisdom, along with others provide the resources required for believers to grow, survive and thrive long term. Development individually and corporately has been divinely designed to occur in a community of those committed to each other.

One statement regarding what we have only introduced occurs in Paul's letter to an Asia Minor church. "We are to grow up in all aspects into Him . . . from whom the whole body, being fitted and held together by what every joint supplies, according to the proper working of each individual part, causes the growth of the body for the building up of itself in love" (Eph. 4:15–16). As someone might say, this is doing it together first class. The body of believers growing up as a whole, thoroughly joined together and making use of what each part provides while being lubricated with love is the picture we see in Ephesians.

Stated simply, we are not to attempt growing or living life as a disciple of Christ alone. We won't make it unscathed and we will never fully experience our potential for long-term change unless we do this together.

For Reflection and Discussion

1. Are you committed to growing together with other Christians because you realize that it is taught so clearly in the Bible and is so necessary?
2. What are you finding to be your greatest difficulties (and often there are many) in trying to grow and find support in your local church or spiritual community?
3. What have been the most helpful contributions you have received from other Christians?
4. Do you feel a need to develop in any area related to an interdependent relationship with other believers?

10

Getting Pruned

"I'm responsible!" Yes, you are, but that's not the whole story. The Lord has a vested interest in you like the gardener who purchases a half dozen shrubs worth a thousand dollars apiece. He will water, prune, maybe do a preplant soil test, fertilize, be sure that insects are controlled and watch for blight damage.

God has far move invested in all of us than we can calculate or imagine. His care for us exceeds that of the best gardener. We are noting one aspect of His care. On the surface it seems harsh and may appear anything but loving.

John 15:2 says that "every branch that bears fruit, He prunes it so that it may bear more fruit." We have all seen piles of leaves, branches and twigs around a bush or tree. This meticulous care is required if the flowering bush or fruit tree is to reach potential productivity or be beautiful.

Drive through apple orchards and you will eventually see an abandoned one. Sprouts line the branches of its trees. Dead limbs are left to limit what little ability such trees have left to produce an apple crop. This orchard will most likely be cut down and burned to make room for a healthy restart. I was responsible for trimming and pruning in our apple orchard so that our trees never got to this state. This is the exact picture given to us in John 15:6. "If anyone does not abide in Me, he is thrown away as a branch and dries up; and they gather them, and cast them into the fire and they are burned."

Like apple trees, we are too valuable to be unattended. If you live in southern Illinois, you see scrub oak. These stunted trees have little value and no one bothers to trim them. In contrast, our status with God and strategic place in the world does not allow us to decline into a state like that of an abandoned orchard. We must be trimmed, pruned or cut back. We must produce what God has ordained long before we were born.

This is what the Lord is speaking about in Psalm 119:75: "I know, O LORD . . . that in faithfulness You have afflicted me." Painful limiting circumstances, which are heartbreaking at times, destructive from our point of view, counterproductive or wasteful, are all reactions from our perspective.

Hebrews pictures the pruning process a little differently. "My son, do not regard lightly the discipline of the Lord . . . Those whom the Lord loves He disciplines, and He scourges every son whom He receives. . . . He disciplines us for our good, so that we may share His holiness. . . . It yields the peaceful fruit of righteousness" (Heb. 12:5–6, 10–11).

Pruning, discipline or child training here is in the context of responsible and wise parenting. No wise parent leaves a child without discipline and neither does the Lord with us. We are more than a shrub or a tree, and we must keep this in mind when the pain of pruning forces its way into our experience.

Proverbs 19:18 says, "Discipline your son while there is hope, and do not desire his death." This verse seems to imply that a parent would have some kind of death wish for a child if discipline is withheld!

Revelation 3:19 places a bigger picture on the same idea. "Those whom I love, I reprove and discipline." Without pruning, disciplining or chastising, the Lord's love toward us could be questioned. "If you are without discipline, of which all have become partakers, then you are illegitimate children and not sons" (Heb. 12:8).

We are urged by the Lord to radical action ourselves: "If your right eye makes you stumble, tear it out and throw it from you; for it is better for you to lose one of the parts of your body, than for your whole body to be thrown into hell. If your right hand makes you stumble, cut it off and throw it from you; for it is better for you to lose one of the parts of your body, than for your whole body to go into hell" (Matt. 5:29–30). The idea is to get rid of or cut out what is counterproductive—the useless or destructive baggage that will always hinder long-term growth. These harsh words place responsibility on us. They require us to take action to deal with sin or distraction in our lives.

This idea of pruning, whether divinely ordained or self-inflicted, is unwanted but needed. We are told how to react in Hebrews 12:12–13: "Therefore, strengthen the hands that are weak and the knees that are feeble, and make straight paths for your feet, so that the limb which is lame may not be put out of joint, but rather be healed." We can't whine, give up, become bitter, or refuse to accept the pruning process which is often disguised in ugly circumstances. We endure while the pruning process helps produce long-term change of a lifetime and validates our experience.

For Reflection and Discussion

1. What is one *discipline experience* that you particularly remember?
2. How do you feel about what we have discussed in this chapter?
3. How would you put the teaching of this chapter in your own words?
4. How would you approach this topic with a new Christian who is going through a hard time and is ready to give up?

Part 3

It's Up to Us

What We Do and How We Cooperate

People of any creed (or no creed at all) can sometimes be described as trying to go up an escalator the wrong way. They keep trying but are never assured of getting to the top. For some of them it seems the escalator is moving faster, and they have to run more rapidly on the moving stairs just to keep pace. Yet they are never able to arrive at the goal of pleasing God, or whatever their aim in life is, as they are trying so desperately to do.

To gain holiness and cooperate with God, some monks over the centuries practiced extreme rigors in fasting, abusing their bodies or depriving themselves in other ways to bring themselves to the desired spiritual level. Some walled themselves into a cell from which they would not exit until they died. It took a lightning bolt from Romans 1:17 to budge Martin Luther out of his monk cell in the Black Cloister in Wittenberg (sometimes called his "tower experience) where he languished and had no peace until the message of grace reached him.

Run-of-the-mill Christians like you and me, while not so radical, may be pedaling quietly but desperately to offer to God what we think He is requiring of us. We need biblical perspective regarding what we are to do and how we should cooperate with the Lord.

Great saints have wrestled and struggled for centuries with how to live the Christian life. What are we supposed to do? How do we know when we are succeeding? What is the balance between what is ours to do and what is God's on our behalf? What are the components of change, what does growing up over a lifetime look like, and is it realistic to expect to get where we should in our Christian experience?

As I mentioned in chapter 2, I gained insights on this when I took an afternoon to look over some of the seven hundred books on the Christian life at a Christian college and another three hundred at our local bookstore. Numerous themes were embedded in these books—products of seeking minds and hearts.

Here are a few of them: theology of the Christian life, self-image and the Christian life, being Christlike, persevering, being thankful, living a life of love, fasting, hungering for God, spiritual disciplines, getting a new you, having a heart for God, commonsense Christianity, warfare in the Christian life, finding the deeper life, desert spirituality, being a Christian pilgrim, abiding in Christ, living in the Spirit, total submission, a manual of spiritual transformation and wholeness.

If it had been a cafeteria, I would have taken a helping of each! This foray into a treasure house of insights for Christian pilgrims gave me some perspective for this book. Of course, these multiple titles make it clear that no one author has the final word on the Christian life.

In this study, we are highlighting *components of living a life with God*. What aspects of the Christian life are part of the biblical picture and make up a reasonable whole? It is a given that no two people will look at it in just the same way. I like to see the ingredients listed on the foods I eat. I noted the more than twenty or more ingredients in cinnamon rolls. The end result is a delicious diet breaker whether you buy them at the grocery store, Dunkin' Donuts or your local bakery. In the same manner, I hope that this book will provide a feast for every person who is hungry to walk with God. This section is the core of the book since it involves how we are to pursue the Christian journey.

We are traveling toward a destination, not arriving, and we are not alone. We are engaged in a process, not achieving the finished product. Just as there are many elements in our lives—such as making dozens of decisions every day, living on many fronts or managing the multiple aspects of our lives (professional, physical, nutritional, financial, family, friendships, community or physical surroundings)—so there are many aspects of the Christian life. So then, let's go for it and consider the elements without tying ourselves to a rigid formula. *We are living a life, not a formula!*

11

Working It Out

What Is Up to Us?

Two books of the New Testament, Galatians and James, are bookends with respect to the idea of working it out and what is up to us in life. Both books are about how Christians look at their responsibilities. They see what Christians are to do from two different perspectives—like opposite-facing bookends. The Galatians were trying to add their efforts to being justified or made right with God. So serious was this error that the apostle Paul responded severely, even invoking a curse on anyone preaching a gospel contrary to what he had preached to them (Gal. 1:6–9).

On the other end were Jewish Christians, to whom James addressed his letter. The way James corrected them was so radical that Martin Luther called the book an epistle of straw worthy of burning. His terrible struggle to be righteous when he himself never could, made the words in James 2:24 seem like heresy when taken out of context: "You see that a man is justified by works and not by faith alone." The Galatian Christians and diaspora Jews to whom James wrote could hardly be further apart. They were bookends! Where do you fall? It must be somewhere in the middle of these two extremes.

With which of the following statements do you identify?

> If the Christian life is going to work, I've got to do my part.
> The Lord expects me to step up to the plate and not make a lot of excuses.
> I've got to give it my best, but I don't have much hope of pleasing the Lord.
> I know He loves me, but He will cut me only so much slack if I keep messing up.

In this section, we look briefly at *working it out—what is up to us?* The fact that the Lord calls us to partner with Him in Christian living, and to give the best to Him who gave His all for us, is a privilege far more than a burden.

We have already noted the principle in Philippians 2:12–13 that we are to work on living as followers of Christ because He is working with, in and for us. In this section, we focus on *our work*. Hundreds of books have been written on the subject. We all have a vocabulary for *working it out*. Each of us could identify with one or more of the following phrases: Put God first, abide in Christ, continue in the faith, persevere, pray all the time, love, forsake sin, be pure, sacrifice, focus on the eternal, follow Him, grow, discipline yourself, confess your sins, trust God, live in or by faith, forget what is behind and focus on the future, run for the finish line, follow what the Bible teaches, place your life on the altar, perform for the audience of One, or live as if this were your final day.

The Bible is our handbook, given to us to guide the course of our lives. The Galatians and the Jewish believers to whom

James wrote lost their way, as we also can. It is imperative that we nail down what we believe and practice it biblically.

We must stay connected to the Bible as we think about responsibilities. In 2 Peter 1:3–11, the apostle gives seven aspects related to *working it out*. Follow these from the passage itself.

1. We begin with a baseline—a rich provision. "His divine power has granted to us everything pertaining to life and godliness. . . . He has granted to us His precious and magnificent promises." We begin and continue our Christian lives with spectacular resources.
2. We are to be *diligent*. Peter begins his instruction by saying, "Now for this very reason also, applying all *diligence*. . . ." Based on the resources we have through faith, we are to build on this reality. Perhaps you can feel Peter's energy in his exhortation. The Christian life demands our best, our focus and consistent effort. Half-heartedness is ruled out at the outset.
3. We work out our Christian life from a foundation of faith. The text says, "In your faith supply. . . ." Through faith in Christ, we have been launched into a new life and faith is the required entry point. What began with faith will continue in faith.
4. According to verse 5, we are to supply, add, or furnish building blocks for our lives as followers of Christ. The Greek word for "supply" conveys the image of a wealthy patron of the arts who lavishly underwrites a production and in so doing displays his wealth. Today we might think of this in terms of being diligent as we equip our lives as believers as we might outfit a dream

home with furnishings. This is what is happening in the passage we are studying here.
5. While Christian living can be viewed as a composite whole with multiple elements, it is also specific and detailed. There are growth or development points which, if not measurable, are at least obvious. The ones which the apostle Peter identifies are:
    - *Virtue* or *moral excellence.* The beginning point is adding the character which mirrors the Lord's. He starts with character from which other characteristics will be developed. "In your faith supply moral excellence," Peter urges.
    - *Knowledge.* Mature Christian living demands the increase of knowledge that goes beyond our emotions, motivations and good intentions. There is no premium on ignorance for the Christian.
    - *Self-control.* Leaders, even though highly qualified and competent people, all too often fail here. Getting old doesn't solve the challenge to self-control. Whatever age or stage we are in, we must be diligent with respect to personal self-control. When this is absent, every other quality is jeopardized.
    - *Perseverance.* Starting well but wiping out or wilting in the back stretch won't work. Building the discipline of perseverance is critical. Peter says, "In self-control, perseverance." Persevering is linked to, or is a function of, self-control. It is self-control extended way down the road.
    - *Godliness.* We are brought back here to the center of the matter. All the specifics lead to the practical reflection of what God is like. It's not supremely

about my flowering into a wonderful human being—it's all about being like God and glorifying Him as I too am brought to glory with Him.
- *Brotherly kindness.* We can't get lost in the general to the extent we miss ground level practice. *Brotherly kindness* involves the way we relate to each other. Being kind when a relative is obnoxious, being considerate when a friend is in deep crisis, helping when they can't help themselves, and any number of other actions or attitudes is the standard the apostle is holding up.
- *Love.* The masterpiece chapter on love in the Bible is 1 Corinthians 13. This final characteristic is absolutely in the right place. All the other things Peter has communicated in this remarkable passage will funnel down in *love*! I find myself reacting to this ending quality with a heart cry, "Lord, have mercy. Despite all your grace and everything Peter has talked about, my heart is so often poverty stricken with respect to love." If we miss this last item, we've missed the rest. Peter has given us an exalted model of Christian experience that is part of long-term change.

We have selected one compact model of growing or developing in our Christian experience. There are numerous others, of course. The great epistle to the Romans ends with several chapters on *working it out.* Look at Romans 12–16 in this light. The second half of Ephesians (chaps. 4–6) emphasizes what is required to *work it out* as well. Paul begins both of these sections with powerful pleas. After the first three chapters, Ephesians 4:1 says, "Therefore I, the prisoner of the Lord, implore you to walk in a manner worthy of the calling with which you have been called." As you read the Bible, you will receive instruction on living out your life with God everywhere!

It is easy to delay throwing the first shovel of dirt, jogging the first lap of a personal training program, or signing up for the first online course that will push your career forward. If you are delaying definitive action steps for life progress as a child of God or just being laissez-faire lazy, here are a couple of action steps to get you going:

- *Pray!* Read chapter 19 on prayer. Start a prayer list and pray with others. Use one of the ideas you find in this chapter. Set aside a few minutes every day and don't stop once you start. Include thanking the Lord for various things as part of your growing prayer life.
- *Use the Bible.* Insist on taking advantage of one of our highest privileges as believers. Chapter 15, "The Bible," discusses what you might do when you devote time reading God's Word and what you should be learning. This chapter will give you practical suggestions if you are beginning this lifelong journey. For those times when you are pressed for time, you will also find help in using the Bible in five minutes or less! Christian bookstores are filled with excellent Bible study materials.
- *Be a part of a fellowship of believers*—a church, Bible study or small group that not only challenges you but pushes you along in specifics of living life with God. Other Christians can become one of the most powerful forces in your life by supporting, encouraging, teaching, and modeling what you learn. Chapter 9 on long-term change together highlights this.

- *Obey!* We can be long on techniques and short on practice. Be intentional about discovering and doing the will of God as you understand it from the Bible and elsewhere. Your responsibility is to know and put into practice what is clearly entrusted to you. Be accountable to someone who can ask you the hard questions and with whom you stay connected as fellow pilgrims. Romans 12:2 provides a classic and compelling exhortation that will help keep you centered. "Do not be conformed to this world, but be transformed by the renewing of your mind, so that you may prove what the will of God is, that which is good and acceptable and perfect." The more we absorb the message of this verse, the greater motivation we find in it.
- *Serve!* If a child is not producing anything by thirty, he is severely stunted. In serving God and others, we also need to be growing. What we integrate, we practice. Steward your time and resources so that you make your life a laboratory of living as a follower of Christ.

The powerful account of Dorcas (Tabitha) and her rising from the dead is recorded in Acts 9:36–42. What made her life distinctive and worthy of recording in the canon of Scripture? It was serving! Hers was not dramatic service that gained notoriety. It was "abounding with deeds of kindness and charity which she continually did" (v. 36). At her wake, "All the widows stood beside him [Peter], weeping and showing all the tunics and garments that Dorcas used to make while she was with them" (v. 39). What a powerful life that was epitomized and memorialized by her serving in ways we might call mundane.

Dorcas had one or more of the spiritual gifts mentioned in Romans 12:4–8 or 1 Corinthians 4:11. Have you figured out yet what yours might be? At the minimum you have at least one special ability that you bring as a member of the body of Christ. Christians who are growing and developing are also serving and using the particular competency entrusted to them.

We have a high and holy calling along with God's people down the centuries to live and work out our relationship with Him in time and space. We need to respond with all that is in us—to *working it out and doing what is up to us!*

For Reflection and Discussion

1. As you read this chapter, did you find yourself feeling excited or motivated to be faithful to the process of *working it out?*
2. How do you relate to this chapter? One could be motivated, feel guilty or frustrated, or be ready to give up. Are you feeling both positive and negative reactions?
3. How would you describe the way in which you are working out your salvation now?
4. If you were e-mailing a younger Christian about working out the dimensions of his or her Christian life, what would you say?

12

Long-Term Changes in Stages

Falling Upward

*G*etting beyond the externals of the Christian life to its essence is the single idea of this chapter. Richard Rohr frames the idea powerfully in *Falling Upward: A Spirituality for the Two Halves of Life* (San Francisco: Jossey-Bass, 2011). He identifies two major tasks in life: "The first task is to build a strong 'container' or identity; the second is to find the contents that the container was meant to hold" (xiii).

The first task involves necessary externals that provide the context for the essentials. What kind of education we pursue, basic relationships, vocation, or where we live provide structure for our lives, but they are not the essentials. "What makes me significant?" "How can I support myself?" and "Who will go with me?" are big "first half of life" questions (1).

We don't get to essentials in a vacuum but do so in time and space. We reach our life fundamentals in a real, tangible, time-based existence.

Rohr says that "the task of the second half of life is, quite simply, to find the actual *contents* that this container was meant to hold and deliver" (1). You can't go to church very long or associate with people who are cutting through the fog of life without being exposed to what it means to separate the important from the essential. The externals frame our lives but are not the essence.

We live in a home formerly occupied by Bob Cook, who left it to become president of King's College in New York. He has been with the Lord for more than twenty years, and his radio programs are still aired. A radio microphone is etched onto his stone grave marker. This helps to epitomize his rather remarkable life as author, educator, radio speaker, and nationally known Christian leader. The radio microphone on his grave stone is an important indicator of who and what he was, but it's not the essential. Who and what we are can't be defined merely by externals, no matter how perfectly they correlate with what is essential about us. Rohr asserts that "the first journey is always about externals, formulas, superficial emotions, flags and badges, correct rituals, Bible quotes. . . . They are all used and needed to create the container" for the second half of life in which we encounter God at a level we could not previously (13).

"Many of us learn to do our 'survival dance' but we never get to our actual 'sacred dance,'" Bill Plotkin says (quoted in Rohr, *Falling Upward*, xviii). We can survive, fulfill ego needs, or find an important life niche but still miss the essential.

I built the book *Dying to Live* around the planting principle stated in John 12:24: "Unless a grain of wheat falls into the earth and dies, it remains alone; but if it dies, it bears much fruit." Getting to what is essential means that any aspect of our external lives, no matter good or pleasurable, is in God's hands. He can remove it—bury it, crush it, allow it to rot—for his own good purposes, if he deems it necessary for our growth. We recognize that God uses the external shell of our lives (as in a kernel of corn) to get to the inestimably valuable kernel!

The apostle John writes of life stages through which God's people move.

> I am writing to you, little children, because your sins have been forgiven you for His name's sake. I am writing to you, fathers, because you know Him who has been from the beginning. I am writing to you, young men, because you have overcome the evil one. I have written to you, children, because you know the Father. I have written to you, fathers, because you know Him who has been from the beginning. I have written to you, young men, because you are strong, and the word of God abides in you, and you have overcome the evil one. (1 John 2:12–14)

One of the interesting aspects of John's paradigm is that "little children," "young men," and "fathers" are each mentioned twice.

The reference to the "little children" is compelling and beautiful. As we noted in chapter 5, the "little children" begin with a new start—sins forgiven and part of a new family. They begin their lifelong journey by knowing or being related to the

Father. According to this chapter's theme, they will be filling their life's container with this knowing, assimilating, or growing process.

John's "young men" stage focuses on the battle or conflict. John's third stage at first glance makes us shake our heads as if we misread the text. He says exactly the same thing twice about the "fathers." Why? It is here in John's enigmatic reference that we get to the depths of *filling our life containers*. John labels fathers in exactly the same way twice because they have nowhere else to go. Their life containers are full! *Knowing the Father includes all the stages, elements, and requirements for a full life container.*

We are filling our lives with what can't be bought, sold, or leased. We understand that the man who customized a car in his youth cannot possibly fill his life container in the second half with a $500,000 luxury or sports car—Rolls Royce, Ferrari, Bentley, or ten-cylinder Audi. He is just upgrading his toys. The same applies to a woman who as a girl had a beautiful and elaborate doll house. It is not enough to upgrade this to a $2 million home as an adult. Her life container has to be filled with what won't be lost when she leaves the planet.

So in the chapters that follow, we turn to those tasks that will occupy us for the rest of our lives as we fill our life containers. This is the real Mount Everest climb! Perhaps we could call it the journey of a thousand lifetimes. In the age to come, faith will become sight, hope too will be seen, and love will be perfected. This journey of getting to that which is essential in God's plan for us comes in stages, but the key is taking the next step and making progress all along the way.

For Reflection and Discussion

1. Have you given thought to life stages for the Christian?
2. Does it make sense that tasks may vary from one stage to the next?
3. What are some of your life tasks now?
4. Are you sensitive to the life stages of Christians with whom you interact so that you don't expect too much or not enough from them?

13

Time to Grow Up

The X Factor

The previous chapter, "Long-Term Changes in Stages: Falling Upward," focused on how our lives take shape in stages. The *X factor* is a term that refers to how time factors into Christian growth, plus other variables that come into play. Antoine de Saint-Exupéry said, "To live is to be slowly born." So many things in our lives are time related. Getting a newborn through the diaper stage and all the way through college is one of the biggest! This week, I spoke with a contractor who mentioned crying over his sixteen-year-old daughter who was pulling out her hair (trichotillomania) and needed a wig. He and his school teacher wife turned quickly to a therapist.

By the time your newborn is married with children, the interminably long process that stretched ahead of you will seem to have passed quickly. By the time the daughter with trichotillomania is thirty, we would anticipate her hair pulling will have become just an embarrassing memory.

What about time-related factors in Christian living—ages, stages and developmental demands? They exist! Stages may be compressed. Some people grow a lot more quickly than others, *but* we all take time to grow. The apostle Paul stayed out of sight early in his career before he blasted onto the stage of the spiritual history of the world. In this same epistle, he urges these Galatian Christians not to stall in an early growth stage.

Peter urges his readers to gain a hunger for "the pure milk of the word" like newborn babies. The lesson is clear. If you are not bottle fed on the Word, you won't grow out of the infant stage. Similarly the writer of Hebrews urges Christians to be "leaving the elementary teaching about Christ" to push on to maturity.

No one is saying in these New Testament epistles that a person should never be a spiritual baby, never need to be bottle fed on milk (elementary teaching) or run before they crawl along as baby Christians. We have noted John's teaching in 1 John 2:12–14 in which he categorizes believers as little children, young people, and mature fathers. Christians are asked to grow up, but they are never asked to skip stages. They are not asked to produce with their own efforts what can only take place with time. Long-term change demands time.

Consider the "10,000-hours rule" that Malcolm Gladwell explores in his book *Outliers: The Story of Success* (New York: Little, Brown and Co., 2008), in which he claims that for freakishly phenomenal performers—from virtuoso violinists to chess grandmasters—it takes about ten thousand hours (roughly ten years) of diligent practice to achieve world-class mastery in a field. This is not to say that anyone who is motivated enough can become an expert in anything they choose to do. Raw talent obviously factors in, along with having the opportunity and right environment in which to develop one's natural ability into genius-level expertise. Yet taking time to grow is never negated. There simply are no shortcuts to maturity, nor for that matter to spiritual maturity in Christ. What is unacceptable is lack of progress.

In *The Spirit of the Disciplines: Understanding How God Changes Lives* (San Francisco: HarperSanFrancisco, 1990), Dallas Willard says with his typical insight,

> No one ever says, "If you want to be a great athlete, go vault eighteen feet, run the mile under four minutes," or "If you want to be a great musician, play the Beethoven violin concerto." Instead, we advise the young artist or athlete to enter a certain kind of overall life, one involving deep association with qualified people as well as rigorously scheduled time, diet, and activity for the mind and body. (8–9)

Christian self-help books, exploring teaching related to the Christian life and counsel for struggling believers, are always in demand. However, attempting to push Christians without accepting time for bottle stages, potty training or adolescent immaturity doesn't work. I felt that I took a lot of time as a baby Christian spilling pabulum on my spiritual bib. But I did grow and develop even though, like a toddler, I sometimes fell more than I stood.

You are no doubt deeply grateful to have started the journey of a lifetime beginning with the new birth, but you probably are not that happy with how far you have come. This chapter is a reminder that *long-term change takes time.* While you may be frustrated with how little you have grown while you are expending every effort you can and exploring every avenue of growth available to you, be encouraged. You are growing. It takes *time.*

And if you are bogged down, still crawling spiritually and using a baby bottle for spiritual nourishment, get on schedule! You have to move on. Paul pushed this bottom-line issue with the Galatian Christians: "My children, with whom I am again in labor until Christ is formed in you" (Gal. 4:19). Using the analogy of delivering a baby underscores the pain and urgency he felt on behalf of these Christians in Asia Minor.

It is clear that there is a general timetable to keep. Our Hebrews author has spoken to the issue in timeless fashion when he says, "For though by this time you ought to be teachers, you have need again for someone to teach you the elementary principles of the oracles of God, and you have come to need milk and not solid food. For everyone who partakes *only* of milk is not accustomed to the word of righteousness, for he is an infant. But solid food is for the mature, who because of practice have their senses trained to discern good and evil" (Heb. 5:12–14).

How long does long-term change take? We are making the point that it takes a lifetime and that stages of development are the norm. It happens in incremental steps. It occurs in our trials. We experience growth as we absorb the Bible more thoroughly. The list goes on but, as in human development, it takes time to grow up and develop. That's the *X factor*.

For Reflection and Discussion

1. Does the idea of developmental stages in the Christian life make sense to you?
2. How would you describe your present stage of Christian experience?
3. What do you recall about your infancy or little child stage?
4. Comment on the following:

a. Have you ever been stuck at a particular stage of your Christian life?
b. Are you on schedule or is there one?

14

Sustained Relationship Over the Long Haul

Hudson Taylor's Spiritual Secret was the book that influenced my life the most dramatically just after my conversion when I was struggling to figure out the Christian life. One incident stands out. He was alone in China. His wife and children were back in England. He was in a cramped living space in the heat of summer and was miserable. On top of all this, he had a liver condition that induced depression.

In this troubled time, he grasped the truth of abiding in Christ as expressed in John 15:5. It changed his life forever, and historically it became a stream that fed into the great nineteenth-century Keswick movement in England. The almost single strain of hundreds of Keswick-type sermons was the message that in some deep crisis we can be driven to an abiding relationship with Christ. We exchange our old way of struggling to a transforming relationship with Him that lifts us beyond what we can produce or work up. Those involved in this Keswick kind of Christian spirituality referred to it as the "exchanged life."

Hudson Taylor arrived in China in 1854, and we still hear his clarion call to abide in Christ. Jean Wilund read *Hudson Taylor's Spiritual Secret*, written by Dr. and Mrs. Howard Taylor (his son and daughter-in-law), and offered this in her Goodreads review online: "My understanding of Jesus' teaching on the vine and the branches in John 15 has been transformed as if a light came on." There are more than a quarter million copies of this book in print today, and this truth is at its core!

Thus John 15:5 is the bull's-eye for this chapter. "I am the vine, you are the branches; he who abides in Me and I in him, he bears much fruit, for apart from Me you can do nothing." I am interested in apple orchards. I grew up in one and took care of it. Seeing apple orchards rolling across the hills in the northern Shenandoah and elsewhere is always an awesome experience for me. After seeing thousands of branches loaded with apples (and sometimes breaking with their weight) or great tracts of land carpeted with grape vines which produce wine for the world, one reality stands out above others and it is the exact point of John 15:5.

The branch has value and can produce only if it remains connected to the tree or vine—a part of it. From there, the miracle development happens. Leaves appear after the winter, blossoms a little later and finally a crop of delicious fruit.

Taking the analogy to its highest point, it would be difficult to underestimate the value that God places on the lives of His children who remain in this connected relationship with Christ. Maturing, growing, changing and being fruitful are a result of staying in a sustained and developing relationship with our Lord. Paul envisions the lives of the Philippians Christians as being *filled with the fruits of righteousness*—a net result of their life experiences. This too is our opportunity, challenge, and privilege. Are you comfortable with how this works?

We are given principles in Revelation 2 and 3 that provide basic insight about living in this present age as Christian exiles. The apostle John conveys the Lord's message to seven churches stretching out in a semicircle east of his place of exile on the island of Patmos in the Aegean Sea. The first and foundational corrective is for the church in Ephesus: "I have this against you, that you have left your first love" (Rev. 2:4). A relationship that has gone stale, a love that has lost its luster, or powerful attraction that is missing its magnetism—they all define the problem.

A young man heading for the ministry spoke with his future father-in-law, who was a seasoned minister and man of God. He said, "John, as you get ready to enter the ministry, I want to give some advice. Stay true to Jesus! Make sure that you keep your heart close to Jesus every day. It's a long way from here to where you're going to go, and Satan's in no hurry to get you" (Farrar, *Finishing Strong*, 6).

What a striking statement! Our Lord will accept nothing less than a sustained and sustainable relationship of love, attraction and devotion. Without it, everything bogs down. It is only reasonable that He says to the church in Ephesus, "Remember from where you have fallen, and repent and do the deeds you did at first; or else I am coming to you and will remove your lampstand out of its place—unless you repent" (Rev. 2:5). The Ephesians had become careless and compromised their early consuming relationship with their Lord. It would be tragic for us to do the same.

We all know that people don't sustain the emotional intensity of that time when they first fell in love—this is not the point.

A deepening love that goes beyond emotional intensity, a fixed focus that lasts year after year, and a sustained relationship that is growing instead of stagnating—that's the idea.

The apostle Paul speaks of his radical commitment to the risen Lord: "But whatever things were gain to me, those things I have counted as loss for the sake of Christ . . . that I may know Him" (Phil. 3:7, 10). He never let go of this vision and held on to it during times when he endured terrible suffering.

The writer of Hebrews (3:12) says it a little more theologically: "Take care, brethren, that there not be in any one of you an evil, unbelieving heart that falls away from the living God." A faith that defies the odds is required and needs to be built up in each of us.

Hosea, the prophet who was married to an unfaithful lover, gives a beautiful and poignant statement of the principle of devotion: "Let us press on to know the LORD" (Hos. 6:3). This prophet's book has heavy overtones of marriage, sexuality, and unfaithfulness. Elsewhere in Scripture the verb *to know* can refer to a sexual relationship (e.g., Gen. 4:1 KJV). Yet as far as God and His people go, the idea here targets spiritual fidelity. The Lord wants us to know Him, and like a husband toward his wife, our God is jealous for our undivided loyalty to Him alone. Uncounted thousands of saints have read this and have had their hearts warmed with longing to "press on to know the LORD."

To continue in a growing relationship to our Lord is not only an absolute minimum, it is also one of the beautiful phenomena a human being can experience. We see it mirrored all the time in human relationships. It is winsome to see it in young couples. Could it be even better to see a tender connected and committed relationship in an old, wrinkled and stooped couple? Their marriage has endured, lasted through multiple challenges, and withstood all the assaults on their relationship as they are walking it out in their final days.

Certainly the countless saints who made it all the way to the end model living out *a sustained relationship over the long haul!* None of us lives this sustained relationship perfectly, but perfection in this life is not the point. Continuing, loving, focusing, and seeking are. Our hungry hearts can guide us in this relational journey along with all the support, resources and encouragements which surround us. Long-term change that is to be our norm will take place like the growth of apples that form on a branch connected to the tree.

For Reflection and Discussion

1. Do you know how to abide in Christ? Is there anything in this requirement that is confusing?
2. Do you need to be clearer about what this means to you in your current stage of Christian living?
3. What is helping you stay in this connected relationship?
4. How might you teach a class on John 15:5 focusing on abiding in Christ?

15

The Bible

Using It!

My everyday use of the Bible began on a cool morning high in the Rockies. A red-haired InterVarsity staff member with a gruff personality was hunched over his Bible at a picnic table. He seemed oblivious to everything else. This was the catalyst that brought together what I had been hearing. The net result is that I have followed a similar practice of daily Bible reading for more than fifty years.

This persuasion, however, is not shared by many Christians today. An associate groaned, "Some church people don't even know that the Bible has verses in it." Visit a cross section of churches with the following questions and you might be disappointed in the answers you receive. "How many Gospels are there? Can you name them? What are the first and last books of the Bible? With what book does the New Testament begin? Why is the Bible essential to the life of a Christian?"

The Bible—If Used

We can't talk about long-term change *without* talking about the Bible, even though some Christians may be woefully ignorant of it. We explore *why* the Bible is essential to long-term growth for the Christian.

There are growth-related natural stages for its use. In 1 Corinthians 4:15, Paul wrote, "I became your father through the gospel." We begin our lifelong journey of faith with the gospel as recorded in the Bible. The Great Commission in Matthew 28 involves "teaching them [people around the world like you and me who respond to the gospel] to observe all that I commanded you" (v. 20). The four Gospels record what our Lord taught and what we are to absorb and obey.

An infant who refuses nourishment is in danger of dying. This analogy is picked up by the apostle Peter (1 Peter 2:2) "Like newborn babies, long for the pure milk of the word, so that by it you may grow." "Pure milk" is essential to a baby's survival, and Peter says to the believer that we too must have this appetite or longing for the Word, Holy Scripture.

There is a time to move on from what nourishes and establishes us in the early stages of Christian experience. The writer of Hebrews says there is a time for "leaving the elementary teaching about the Christ, . . . not laying again a foundation . . . of instruction about washings and laying on of hands, and the resurrection of the dead and eternal judgment" (Heb. 6:1–2). He is saying that the fundamentals of what feeds us early on are irreplaceable. However, we must move on to what is demanded in the following stages of our experience.

If we are to get where we need to go, some kind of boundaries must be established so that we do not drift along. Jesus says in John 17:17, "Sanctify them in the truth; Your word is truth." The Bible is that purifying, preserving influence that positions us to live as required for a life that wins. Like medicine, we must use it for it to work.

Early and middle stages of Christian life demand study or attention to God's Word as our guidebook, textbook and manual of instructions. For most of us, instruction received in church or small group settings is a part of this process. We cannot be responsible or fully eligible without attention to study of Scripture. Paul gives us a classic statement about the place and function of the Bible for the believer. "All Scripture is inspired by God and profitable for teaching, for reproof, for correction, for training in righteousness; so that the man of God may be adequate, equipped for every good work" (2 Tim. 3:16–17).

We are to be provided with *teaching* (what we need for living); *reproof* (a wakeup call as needed); *correction* (course corrections needed along the way); and *training in righteousness* (in holy living). The end result is that we are *adequate* for the demands placed upon us, God's people, who are children of light and *equipped* or able to perform the tasks which are critically needed in our generation and life span.

Psalm 119 exemplifies the use of Scripture in a more mature stage of life. Each month, I anticipate reaching Psalm 119 in my reading cycle. It is a lavish and extravagant praise of Scripture. It is the longest chapter of the Bible and reaches spectacular heights of literary excellence.

The entire psalm is in eight-verse stanzas. Each stanza celebrates Scripture with every verse of the eight beginning with the particular letter of the Hebrew alphabet. In the first stanza, each verse begins with *alef*, the first letter in the Hebrew alphabet, and so it goes along for the remaining seven verses in the stanza. What happens each month for me occurs daily for the psalmist: "Seven times a day I praise You, because of Your righteous ordinances" (v. 164).

Over the months and years, I have marked up this psalm in whatever Bibles I have used. It is like a multicarat diamond in which different facets light up whenever I look at it through the lens of my changed circumstances or soul state.

This psalm speaks of the blessedness of Word keepers, how we have our praise elevated when the Word saturates us, the critical call to meditation, insatiable longing for His communication to us, the reviving influence of it, the absolute reliability and stability of what is revealed in His inspired message to us, the place of affliction in driving the Scriptures more deeply into our being, grief at those who ignore biblical precepts, how delight in the Bible sustains one during affliction, determination never to let go of what God has revealed, the Scriptures as the greatest delicacy available to a human being, its function as lamp and light, and the Word as a sustaining influence throughout our lives. This is a beginning list!

The Bible Used!

The qualifier *if used* should never apply to our use of the Bible. Long-term, permanent commitment to being *users* is required!

It seemed fitting or necessary to end this chapter with practical suggestions. A Christian leader with fifty years' experience told me that I would be surprised at how few men who are serious Christians read the Bible consistently. No doubt there are many reasons such as spiritual laziness, severe time pressures, or "tried it and it didn't work." For our purposes, we will give everybody the benefit of the doubt and work with someone who is ready and wants to know how to get started.

We include just a few. Take your pick or try something with which you are already familiar. Try one and discard it if doesn't work well. Find one that fits you. In the *Life Serve Mentoring Program*, we use at least twenty study methods and several five-minutes-or-less approaches for Christians in the marketplace.

1. *Proverbs for the day* works well with so many. Since there are thirty-one chapters in Proverbs, a person can just go to the Proverb chapter for the day of the month. The sixth day of the month means chapter six of Proverbs.

    Try this: Choose your Proverb chapter. Take thirty seconds to find a verse in the chapter that interests you. What is one thing that it is saying to you? Respond in some way, such as praying about it, giving thanks, jotting a note to yourself or making sure you remember the thought for the day.

    A note: Two or three barbers were taking a quick break, Bibles in hand. I asked them to do this exercise. They did so in less than two minutes and I asked them to close their Bibles. They seemed shocked at how quick and effective it was.

2. *Grab a verse* is the same idea as we used for Proverbs. Have you ever thought, "I don't have time to eat breakfast," and at the last minute decided to grab a glass of orange juice and a piece of toast folded over with some jam in it? In the same way, don't give up entirely when you have insufficient time to conduct what you consider a "proper" time with God.

    Look quickly over a group of Psalms such as Psalms 55–59 and select a verse or so such as 55:22, 56:13, 57:7–8, or 59:16. The verse you choose will likely provide orange juice (quick energy and vitamins), toast (fuel for morning activities) and jam (sending you off with a good taste in your mouth) if you focus on it for a few moments. There are 150 psalms and some people take a psalm block daily—five psalms for any day of the month. (Example: The fifth day of the month would mean Psalms 25–29 as your group for the day.)

3. *Brief passages.* We think of BP (British Petroleum) as a supplier of fossil fuel energy products. You fill your tank at one of the stations branded with the green and yellow colors. God gives energy to fuel our lives as well. A primary fuel source is the living, written Word of God, the Bible. The brief passages used for this project are intended to help jump-start your day.

Here are a few passages to try: Job 1:20–22; Psalm 3; Psalm 37:23–24; 1 Corinthians 15:51–58; 1 John 5:13–17; Ephesians 4:25–32; Revelation 22:1–5.

Read the passage you select (*into your tank*), review or think it over (*into your carburetor*), to get something you need—challenge, promise, counsel, call to change or correct something, an encouragement, etc. (*"fires" in your combustion chamber*); power up for the day (*the car actually runs!*).

4. *Daily devotional book.* Numerous daily devotional guides are published. Your church may have copies or your Christian bookstore should have a sampling of them. Most denominations issue their own. Interdenominational resources are available such as the long-standing classic, *Our Daily Bread* published by RBC Ministries (formerly known as Radio Bible Class). Another standard devotional is Scripture Union's *Discovery*, whose online description says it is designed

so "each day's reading covers 10–15 verses, just the right amount for people on the go." The format often involves a story or illustration, the Bible passage under consideration, the verse for the day, an inspirational thought or other feature.
5. *A small group* has helped launch many into their personal use of the Bible.
6. *Ask a pastor or other knowledgeable person* for suggestions on how you might use the Bible. You might be surprised at their excitement over your request.
7. *Contact Life Serve* for resource possibilities.

For Reflection and Discussion
1. How would you describe your relationship to the Bible?
2. Do you know *how* to use the Bible?
3. If not, what could you do to figure it out? What changes would you be willing to make?
4. What has your use of the Bible produced for you?

16

Spiritual Disciplines

A few of us can remember when we did not have a TV in our home. Children who have grown up with a TV have watched thousands of commercials and hundreds of hours of programs and videos. The average young person or adult today would feel lost without a TV and iPhone, iPad, computer, DVD player, or social media.

Richard Foster says that "our Adversary majors in three things: noise, hurry, and crowds. If he can keep us engaged in 'muchness' and 'manyness,' he will rest satisfied" (*Celebration of Discipline: The Path to Spiritual Growth* [San Francisco: Harper & Row, 1988], 15). Our Lord escaped all three when, as the Gospels report on more than one occasion, He left the house before others got up and went out alone to pray.

We also need to include a fourth that can make it impossible to come apart as our Lord did—our high-tech devices. We can carry the world in our pocket via a cell phone or bring along fifty *favs* with an iPod. We can go to a remote location as our Lord did when He left before sunrise and still be so wired that we find it impossible to disconnect for a few hours.

Perhaps we need a "sabbath rest" from our devices at least once a week, if not for some part of every day.

No one would disagree that the digital age, which notably occupies the tiniest sliver of the time line of human history, has its advantages. One that I appreciate is the ease with which a large family like ours can stay in contact when we are far apart. However, the debilitating downside of our overcommunicating world needs to be counterbalanced. A serious practice of spiritual disciplines is particularly important today for many reasons. They can lessen some the negative and destructive tendencies of living in a high-tech world.

Few of us would disagree with William Ralph Inge's claim in that "no labour is better expended than that which explores the way to the treasure-houses of the spirit, and shows mankind where to find those goods which are increased by being shared, and which none can take from us" (*Personal Religion and the Life of Devotion* [New York: Longmans, Green and Co., 1924], 18). We may be okay with the "treasure-houses of the spirit" idea, but we are probably also a little conflicted by this concept. "Sure I would like to be more spiritual or be a better Christian and have a deeper spiritual life, but what skills do I need to find it? Will these disciplines fit my lifestyle or are they remnants from the Dark Ages when monks wore hair shirts? Will I have to become reclusive? Will my results be so meager that I will find my attempts futile and discouraging?" Admittedly, the term *spiritual disciplines* feels a little foreboding, like sky diving.

Let's start with basic ideas and stay there in this chapter. If you are ready to go further or even if you are already down the road of using spiritual disciplines, you can find numerous reputable resources online or in your local Christian bookstore.

A grandson-in-law said he was reallocating his time in morning devotions so that he spent more time in prayer. That is a spiritual discipline in motion. Our Lord practiced this in an unforgettable way in an incident recorded in Mark 1:35. "In the early morning, while it was still dark, Jesus got up, left the house, and went away to a secluded place, and was praying there."

The person who decides for the first time to pause and pray meaningfully before a meal may be opening a door to a treasure house of the spirit—the practice of praise. In a recent book titled *Praise in the Time Stream of Our Lives* I reported the results of devoting myself to the practice of praise in my daily life. This tremendous opportunity confronts us many times every day. We just need to practice the obvious, commonsense practice of giving thanks.

A spiritual discipline is any practice that encourages or develops our relationship with God. An accumulation of wisdom and insights for the practice and understanding of spiritual disciplines has grown over the centuries. I define them this way: Spiritual disciplines are those practices which encourage, facilitate and develop our lives with God personally and in the community and world in which we live.

To put the idea in a broader perspective, Donald Coggan said, "I go through life as a transient on his way to eternity, made in the image of God but with that image debased, needing to be taught how to meditate, to worship, to think" (quoted in Foster, *Celebration of Discipline*, 1). Foster says that spiritual disciplines help us "place ourselves before God so that He can transform us. . . they are a way of sowing to the Spirit" (*Celebration of Discipline*, 7). Practicing spiritual disciplines is one of our greatest opportunities as believers.

The challenge of living a life in which we find spiritual treasure comes with issues such as the cost to be paid, finding the way to do it, or managing priorities which demand too much of us. Evelyn Underhill said, in essence, that spiritual achievement carries a price tag but never as much as it is worth. Spiritual disciplines need to be integrated into our lives if we are to expect long-term changes that will make our lives fulfilling in the best sense, strategic and distinctively glorifying to God.

For our purposes, we address this timeless way of life with simplicity while trusting that those who are already on the way will continue and those who feel fire and passion will break down all the obstacles that keep them from it. In *Spiritual Disciplines for the Christian Life* (Colorado Springs: NavPress, 1991), Donald Whitney puts our thoughts together when he says,

> It's not uncommon for an accomplished musician to be able to sit down in front of a new piece of music and play it through without a hitch. He makes it seem easy, as if it required no effort. Yet, the "freedom" to play with such skill comes only after years of disciplined practice. In the same way, the freedom to grow in godliness—to express Christ's character through your own personality—is in large part dependent on a deliberate cultivation of the spiritual disciplines found in God's Word. Far from being legalistic, restrictive, or binding, as they are often perceived, the spiritual disciplines are actually the means to unparalleled spiritual liberty. (97)

Adele Calhoun makes a valuable contribution in her outstanding book, *Spiritual Disciplines Handbook: Practices That Transform Us* (Downers Grove, IL: InterVarsity Press, 2005). While authors use different approaches, they open the door and let the wind of spiritual disciplines rush in. Calhoun categorizes the disciplines under seven headings. They can belong to those who spend much time in solitude or others who live in the rapids of a harried life. She takes the word *worship* and uses each letter as a heading for seven categories of spiritual practices:

Worship
Open myself to God
Relinquish the false self
Share my life with others
Hear God's Word
Incarnate the love of Christ
Pray

Calhoun provides a bank vault full of ideas and practical means to practice the disciplines.

In *Celebration of Discipline*, Richard Foster delineates the disciplines differently. He uses Inward Disciplines (meditation, prayer, fasting, study); Outward Disciplines (simplicity, solitude, submission, service); and Corporate Disciplines (confession, worship, guidance, celebration) as his paradigm.

We should not let our perceptions, confusion or apprehensions hold us back. We can begin by selecting those disciplines with which we resonate, that stimulate a hunger for more or point to a missing element in the way we are living. We can begin by including practices we have missed or neglected.

Be selective! Be patient! These two principles will help us pull the material of this chapter down for real life practice.

Be selective! Don't try to practice every discipline mentioned in this chapter at once. You will be frustrated and will likely give up.

You could choose from the basic disciplines we treat in this book. *Using the Bible* as a fundamental discipline for Christian

Spiritual Disciplines

living is highlighted in chapters 7 and 15. *Doing life with other Christians* is described as a base-line practice in chapter 9. *Practicing prayer* is a required discipline from spiritual infancy to developed maturity. Read chapter 19 to get a better hold on the practice of prayer. *Meditating on the Bible* is so important that we devote all of chapter 17 to this it. When it comes to meditation, just start somewhere! *Practicing praise* as a way of life will raise your life to a new level. My book *Praise in the Time Stream of Our Lives* is written to encourage you in this discipline.

Be patient! You are not sprinting, running a mile or a half marathon. You are working on the rest of your life. This means you may falter or fall off the wagon into sloppiness or sloth from time to time. Be patient. Over the course of your life, you can and will build into your life what wasn't there before—*your package of spiritual disciplines.*

Hosea 6:3, mentioned in the previous chapter, was used as a key verse when Jo Ann and I attended Columbia International University in South Carolina. This verse says, "Let us know, let us press on to know the LORD. . . . He will come to us like the rain, like the spring rain watering the earth." The idea of knowing, pressing on and experiencing the presence of the Lord in my life like rain in a desert creates a desire in me I can hardly express when I read the verse. Spiritual disciplines point the way! Spiritual disciplines are an integral part of long-term change—like doing pushups when you are getting in shape. *Meditation*, a spiritual discipline of the ages, is up next!

For Reflection and Discussion

1. What is your definition of a spiritual discipline? Was it helpful to consider a more expanded view of spiritual disciplines than you might have previously?
2. Which disciplines are most important to you?

3. Is there a spiritual discipline or practice that you feel you are missing or are not finding the means to practice?
4. Would you like to make spiritual disciplines a more important part of your life in the future? If so, how might you do this?

17

Meditation

The Timeless Discipline

Meditation is a fundamental discipline which is urged upon us in Scripture. Today we are memory midgets when it comes to the Bible, and meditation deprived. Biblical meditation is a millennia-old practice. If you have never done so before, "Stop. Don't pass go" until you have seriously considered *meditation* in this chapter.

Two meditation mandates have anchored my heart for thirty-plus years. I memorized them early in my Christian experience. The first, "This book of the law shall not depart from your mouth, but you shall meditate on it day and night, so that you may be careful to do according to all that is written in it; for then you will make your way prosperous, and then you will have success" (Josh. 1:8). So much is on the surface here—the Word is to be supreme, demanding consideration in heart and mind day and night. None of us does this perfectly, but the command given to Joshua should be met with hunger and determination to do it as best we can. What we internalize with meditation is to be externalized in practice. We in turn are promised a significant level of success versus success without significance.

The next major statement is addressed to the *blessed person* of whom it is said that "his delight is in the law of the LORD, and in His law he meditates day and night. He will be like a tree firmly planted by streams of water, which yields its fruit in its season and its leaf does not wither; and in whatever he does, he prospers" (Ps. 1:2–3). Here, our inner thought and reflective life follow our delight. Some of us need to acquire the discipline of delight (joy, pleasure, enjoyment, relish) in Scripture to push us on to what follows—meditation! This practice connects us to what is life-sustaining.

Have you ever picked up an English copy of the Qur'an and marveled that select Muslim children are called on to memorize the whole of it when they frequently don't even understand the classical Arabic in which it is written? Many Muslims have come to faith when they find how much superior the Bible is to the Qur'an and when their hunger for a God who loves us personally and removes our sin and guilt is met. How can we treat memorization of the Bible so carelessly when it enables us to access God's Word more deeply?

I sometimes help a person "break the meditation barrier." The idea is to try the discipline of harvesting the benefit from what has been memorized by thinking about, reviewing, and reflecting on the verse or passage until you gain a valuable insight you have never considered previously.

I have a five-minute drive from my home to office or coffee shop in downtown Glen Ellyn. Recently I was meditating on the Colossians prayer in 1:9–12 as I drove and was gripped with the phrase "filled with the knowledge of His will" in verse 9. I was riveted by the reality that we can gain a grasp of His will even while living in a culture that is often like a barren desert devoid of this knowledge. I prayed earnestly for Christians around the world that we as a people would be filled with the knowledge of His will. In this way, we will be like wells or oases in a desert. I was still gripped with this prayer item later in the day. A normally unfocused five minutes made the difference.

Psalm 119 is one of the most powerful chapters of the Bible for me. I visit it monthly with anticipation. I monitor the several references to both meditation and affliction. The psalmist says, "I will meditate on Your precepts and regard Your ways. . . . Your servant meditates on Your statutes. . . . But I shall meditate on Your precepts. . . . My eyes anticipate the night watches, that I may meditate on Your word" (vv. 15, 23, 78, 148)."

The Israelites wrestled with the process of meditation. Two Hebrew verbs, *hagah* and *siyach,* are the vehicles for meditation. A related word is *zakar*, "to remember." What we implant firmly by meditation will be effectively remembered. *Zakar* is Moses' word in Deuteronomy for the people to remember what he was teaching (Peter Toon, *From Heart to Mind: Christian Meditation Today* [Grand Rapids: Baker, 1987], 23–24). Mediation for the Israelites was a matter of life and death as far as maintaining the covenant blessings was concerned. If they forgot about God and His words of life, the nation faced eventual moral collapse, national calamity, and the slavery of exile (see Deuteronomy 27–30; Josh. 1:8; Ps. 1).

The Hebrew concept for meditation is powerful and expressive. In *Satisfy Your Soul: Restoring the Heart of Christian Spirituality* (Colorado Springs: NavPress, 1999), Bruce Demarest explains that "[u]tter, groan, ponder. . . . muse, rehearse (in the mind), [and] contemplate" are all connotations of the process we label "meditation" (133–34). Meditation "involves deep, repetitive reflection" and permits the Holy Spirit to activate the Word of

God within. We *give "attention with intention"* when we meditate, and as Puritan pastor Richard Baxter put it this classic practice of millennia helps "*open the door between head, heart, life and practice*" (133–35, emphasis added).

"Meditation is the devotional practice of pondering the words of a verse or verses of Scripture with a receptive heart. Meditation is 'the digestive faculty of the soul.' . . . *Meditate* is taken from the Latin root word, *medicalus*, from which we get our world 'medicine,' and medicine, we know, never does any good in the bottle, it has be taken internally" (Campbell McAlpine, *The Practice of Biblical Meditation: Discovering a Deeper Spirituality through the Bible* [Tonbridge, England: Sovereign World, 2002], 74, 80).

In *The Living Reminder: Service and Prayer in Memory of Jesus Christ* (1977; repr., San Francisco: HarperSanFrancisco, 1998), Henri Nouwen speaks with passion about what meditation on God's Word involves:

> If we really want to be living memories . . . the word of God must be engraved in our hearts; it must become our flesh and blood. . . . It means meditating and ruminating on God's Word—chewing it or, as the Psalmist puts it, 'murmuring' it day and night. In this way the Word of God can slowly descend from our mind into our heart. . . . This meditation on God's Word is indispensable if we want to be reminders of God and not of ourselves. . . . Since the greatest news is that the Word has become flesh, it is indeed our . . . vocation and obligation to continue this divine incarnation through daily meditation on the Word. (69)

Jeremiah speaks to the same point! "Your words were found and I ate them, and Your words became for me a joy and the delight of my heart; for I have been called by Your name, O LORD God of hosts" (Jer. 15:16). Stop unless you have learned to "eat" Scripture, that is, *meditate*!

In my own experience over the years, I have used many memory cards and several systems. My most recent is a synthesis using three sets of three-by-five cards which include Old Testament, Gospels, and Epistles. On them I have several dozen verses that I want to be able to access immediately from memory. So often some special truth emerges from the verse I am working on that day that just fits my life. *Now* is perhaps your opportunity to upgrade your practice of this millennia-old practice of meditation.

Don't be intimidated if this is a new discipline. Begin by selecting two or three verses to memorize. Record them on something that you can take with you or post where you will see it. Think about the verses as you drive, wash dishes or carry on normal activities. Be patient and expect the results to more than repay your effort.

For Reflection and Discussion

1. What was most challenging or meaningful in this chapter?
2. How was your understanding concerning meditation broadened?
3. Describe your experience with meditation and its value.
4. How might you use this strategic discipline with greater profit?

18

The Promises!

All of us understand to some extent the importance of the Bible in the life of a Christian, but the *promises in the Bible* are sometimes not well recognized as special treasures.

Promises personalized for me became a reality early in my journey. My conversion experience was born out of a personal crisis when it appeared that the Lord was letting me know, "It's now or never!" My baby stage after conversion was a continual struggle. I was defeated so often and seemed always to be spilling "baby food on my spiritual bib."

During these up and down days, a thread of verses from Old to New Testaments became living, real, and foundational and remain so to this day. Psalm 66 gives a litany of severe trials such as being refined in the fire, the enemy riding over us (one wrongly placed hoof and it would be over!), being caught in a net, and going through fire and water.

The end result of all this torment and trial is stated like this, "Yet You brought us out into a place of abundance" (v. 12). I visualized crawling through a slimy sewer-like pipe and seeing a light ahead. I reached it and crawled out into a beautiful meadow gleaming in the sunlight. "That is the way I will end up after all these sewer-pipe experiences," I said to myself. I hung onto this hope from Psalm 66 which pictured vividly what I was going through but also what I could expect ahead.

My next connector in the chain of promises is found in 2 Corinthians 2:14. "But thanks be to God, who always leads us in triumph in Christ, and manifests through us the sweet aroma of the knowledge of Him in every place." This link of the chain helped me hold on during times in the pit. *Victory* is what my end experience will be! I exulted in this hope while living in my dark circumstances, which included supporting a family of six on an uncertain income. My final place of refuge is found in 1 Peter 5:9–10: "Knowing that the same experiences of suffering are being accomplished by your brethren who are in the world. After you have suffered for a little while, the God of all grace, who called you to His eternal glory in Christ, will Himself perfect, confirm, strengthen and establish you." It was so powerful for me. I felt a part of this great global process of suffering that my brothers and sisters were experiencing all around the world which I too was sharing.

The triumphal results noted in this passage resonated with me as I floundered. Perfected, confirmed, strengthened and established would be the net result of what I was laboring through in dark isolation.

I like to think that particular promises in the Bible have our names written on them. Get in the Bible and claim every one that has your name on it! Stated another way—the Holy Spirit intends that selected promises in the Bible are meant to be personalized and made ours in some special way during our life journeys. It has happened to millions of God's people through the centuries.

We often receive God's promises when we are in a state that makes them seem quite improbable. Joseph was given his promise in a dream that he would become superior in his family. Shortly thereafter he was sold into slavery and ended up in a dungeon. There he had the choice of believing his circumstances—a hopeless life in a dungeon or God's promise of an exalted future. He chose the invisible promise over his all too real circumstances. We too must cling to the promise(s) that have become ours when there is not much hope of them coming to pass.

The same happened with Abraham and Sarah. They were entrusted with the amazing privilege of initiating the promised line by which the entire world would be blessed. This included Messiah's coming as Emmanuel—God with us. Abraham was close to 100 years old and Sarah about 90. A child was impossible and the promise of God to them was now virtually unfulfillable. "Yet, with respect to the promise of God, he did not waver in unbelief but grew strong in faith, giving glory to God, and being fully assured that what God had promised, He was able also to perform" (Rom. 4:20–21). He is given as an example of someone who hung on to God's promise when it appeared to be mocking him.

The promises of God are not only a luxury to be used but a sacred trust to be received, held onto and believed when the immediate evidence seems to veto them. A solemn message says, "Therefore, let us fear if, while a promise remains of entering his rest, any one of you may seem to come short of it." The passage continues by saying "the word they heard did not profit them, because it was not united by faith in those who heard." A concluding statement says, "They shall not enter My rest" (Heb. 4:1–3). God's promises demand our commitment, not a sloppy acquiescence that evaporates when we are tested. Second Peter 1:4 is an exclamation point to the discussion on the promises of God. "He has granted to us His precious and magnificent promises, so that by them you may become partakers of the divine nature." The promises are described in superlatives—precious! magnificent! catalyst for transformation! It reminds me of a kid's song that was popular years back. "Every promise in the book is mine, every chapter, every verse, every line." You may be reacting to this chapter with enthusiasm but also saying, "I don't know where to start. No single verse is coming to mind. Should I choose a promise I like or one that gives me assurance in some basic area like God's love or one that guarantees my place in heaven?"

The basic answer is, "Choose one. Get started. Do something!" Here are a few choices that could give you your first one if you need a boost. Verses like John 3:16 or 1 John 5:13 assure us of our salvation. Second Timothy 3:16–17 gives us basic truth regarding the place the Bible should have in our lives. Psalm 97:11 is a good choice if you are going through a dark time in your life. Second Corinthians 2:14 is great if you are wondering whether you are going to make it or survive a crisis. Proverbs 3:5–6 or James 1:5 have been claimed by many who are saying, "I need guidance at this time in my life." Christians have used verses from Psalm 23 frequently for comfort or assurance. Second Corinthians 1:3–4 are *comfort verses* as well. Romans 1:16 or Revelation 3:20 give us confidence that God will respond to us when we come to Him for salvation. Choose John 14:16 for your promise relating to the presence of the Holy Spirit with you.

Promises related to numerous topics such as the second coming of Christ (chap. 26) are scattered throughout the

Bible. Be alert for verses that are especially meaningful to you. The very few verses we have recommended suggest that the Bible is a treasure store of promises that help establish us in our faith, comfort us when needed, instruct us in truth which is basic, or assure us when we are threatened by storms or crises in our lives.

Whether in the most general terms or the most specific ("I believe the Lord has given me a promise for what I am going through"), promises entrusted to believers are treasures. We can be losers only if we neglect, treat them carelessly, or assign them the most minimum value. *The promises!* They are ours for the living!

For Reflection and Discussion

1. Can you think of at least one promise in the Bible that has been significant to you?
2. What is important to you from this consideration of the biblical promises we have been given?
3. Have you neglected the impact these promises are supposed to have on you?
4. Going forward, consider compiling a short list of promises (if you haven't already) that you would like to be a more significant part of your life.

19

Prayer

Foundation of Christian Experience

Why do you and I struggle with our praying as we do? Is it because we wonder how much our prayers get answered or are even heard by the Lord? "How can He hear what I am thinking when I pray or decipher my prayer when a million others are praying too? Sometimes it feels like I am just talking into the air! I wish I could feel His presence and love a little more—like when I bend down and put my arm around a child and hold her close when she is crying and trying to tell me what is bothering her."

We have our lists of things that discourage praying. Psalm 66:18 offers one such caution—the idea that if I am permitting some kind of sin in my heart, I am wasting my time in praying. A sense of guilt pervades time set aside for prayer. For others it is busyness when other things push out meaningful, concentrated time. Racing, distracting, or competing thoughts make praying a losing cause for some. Have you had to admit, as I have with embarrassment, something like this: "I don't like to pray as I should. It's not a pleasant task for me. It's not something I look forward to"? This condition led me to several months of praying about my praying!

With all the things that push us away or prevent praying, there are more that encourage us. Romans 8:26–27 has inspired me for a long time: "The Spirit also helps our weakness; for we do not know how to pray as we should, but the Spirit Himself intercedes for us with groanings too deep for words; and He who searches the hearts knows what the mind of the Spirit is, because He intercedes for the saints according to the will of God." When it comes to praying, our weakness or frailty is acknowledged right up front. Not even knowing how to pray or articulate what is so deeply or painfully inside us, however, is made intelligible to the Father by the Holy Spirit, who communicates for us what we can't put into words. Our longing is constructed into a prayer, and it becomes part of how the Spirit Himself is praying according to God's will on our behalf or through us.

There is something particularly encouraging about the prayer sections of James. Instruction to pray during suffering or sickness, to confess one's sins and find healing are provided here. The nugget I am referring to is connected to Elijah's career. He prayed earnestly and it didn't rain for three and one-half years! Our prayer promise exemplified by Elijah is that "the effective prayer of a righteous man can accomplish much" (James 5:16). We don't have to figure it out. We are just to accept the fact that the prayers of righteous saints around the world are used to "accomplish much," and we are part of this reality.

One of my sons and I came up with the same question independently. To what extent has God answered the prayers of thousands of monks and nuns in monasteries and convents over the centuries to change history for good? How is He using ours today as well? It is God's to know and ours to practice—prayer in faith that we are in some way partnering with God in His program for our day.

When the great apostle asks to be supported by the prayers of the Ephesian Christians, he says, "With all prayer and petition pray at all times in the Spirit." Just keep praying is what he is asking us to do. Don't be discouraged or stop. Just keep praying!

How do we go about praying? For what do we pray? Each of us is different, but the basics are similar and the Bible has a lot to say. For example, praying for others during crisis times when we are so helpless to intervene is a great resource for them and ourselves. Paul on one occasion said, "I know that this will turn out for my deliverance through *your prayers* and the provision of the Spirit of Jesus Christ" (Phil. 1:19).

Paul, along with Silas, was in a terrifically bad situation in Philippi. They were thrown into jail and beaten with rods—something almost inconceivable for us. Their extreme discomfort was increased when they were put in stocks without the means of starting the process of healing for their wounds. With his Philippian experience behind him, Paul was once again under house arrest in Rome and calling for needed support.

Note how we partner with the Lord in our crisis praying. Paul was assured that the active intervention of the Holy Spirit coupled with the prayers of the Philippians would work together and be a part of God's plan and provision for his life. We too are to pray for our fellow believers during their crises, not only as an obligation but also with expectation.

First Thessalonians 5 provides two concise aspects of prayer. The first can be puzzling: "Pray without ceasing" (v. 17). Obviously, we can't be devoting ourselves to praying all the time to the exclusion of what we must give our attention to. However, prayer can be consistent, thoroughly incorporated in our daily lives, an attitude that surrounds what we do and experience. This may include responding to an unexpected urge to pray for someone or something. This can be a directive from the Holy Spirit.

What is stated in the next verse may be a new insight: "In everything give thanks; for this is God's will for you in Christ Jesus" (v. 18). Giving thanks is a part of our unceasing praying. This pervasive practice of praise is to be part of all our circumstances. "In everything" is the idea. The circumstance, even though dark or tragic, is not to stem the flow of praise. God, His works, His provision or His plan calls for praise even though our hearts might be broken in the short term. If we are in a delightful period or episode of life, praise becomes a natural expression and reaction to the joy or happiness we are enjoying.

Prayer is intended to cover a wide spectrum. We are not to be stingy as if it would be wasteful to include too much. Even though it may be impossible to measure or observe the difference prayer makes, Paul says in a pastoral epistle, "I urge that entreaties and prayers, petitions and thanksgivings, be made on behalf of all men, for kings and all who are in authority" (1 Tim. 2:1–2). Our prayers are to pervade the breadth and length of the world in which we live.

We are given specific requests and patterns for prayer. Four of Paul's prayers are recorded in his church epistles. I love each but particularly appreciate the first of these in Ephesians 1:15–20.

- He requests that the Ephesian Christians would have a very special "spirit of wisdom and of revelation in the

knowledge of Him" (v. 17). The idea that the experiential knowledge of God would be natural and deeply integrated in their lives breathes fresh air into my heart.
- The ascending scale of this prayer continues with the request that we might be gripped with the reality of the hope of our calling (v. 18). Being mastered by the hope that God has put in front of us is a powerful driving force for Christians.
- The next petition in the last part of verse 18 is almost too much to believe! This request sounds preposterous: that we are to be captivated by the fact that we are the Lord's supreme treasures—His inheritance and glory! Internalizing this life-changing reality will push beyond sloppy, third-rate, self-centered living.
- Finally, he prays that we might grasp and find in some way "the surpassing greatness of His power toward us who believe" (v. 19). The measure or standard of this reality is what "He brought about in Christ, when He raised Him from the dead and seated Him at His right hand in the heavenly places" (v. 20). Resurrection power is to operate with us as it did with Christ, and Paul integrates this amazing idea into his prayers.

We are learning "to pray big" here. We are led beyond necessary yet temporal prayers that deal with health, marriage and family, or job issues to life's ultimate concerns. Praying must be a priority for us, but we also need to be instructed in how we pursue our praying.

This is only one of the apostle Paul's prayers for members of the churches that he carried in his heart. This one is spectacular and we have only gotten to the surface of it. Another is found in the third chapter. Another is on behalf of the Philippians and the final one for the Colossians.

These prayers can help guide our prayers along with numerous other instructions and examples available to us in the Bible.

Long-term change without prayer? It doesn't exist! This chapter should function as a stimulus or call to prayer. However it might apply to each of us, let's be steadfast in a life of prayer. Our questions or hindrances that challenge serious commitment to praying may remain. Whatever the case, we are to pray! We can get help, instruction, support, or divine enablement to do so.

For Reflection and Discussion

1. How would you describe your practice of prayer?
2. What challenged you in this section?
3. Should you devote some time to a biblical study on prayer or read a book(s) on this theme?
4. What changes would you like to make in your prayer life?

20

Habits of Holiness

I remember a Christian leader saying to men, "You don't want to wait to establish your behavior principles until a woman knocks on the door of your hotel room. It may be too late then!" Have you noticed that sometimes your fiercest temptations come when you are at your lowest or most vulnerable state?

Like Gatorade, if habits of holiness are not *in you*—integrated over months and years of practice—you may be in trouble. Long-term change doesn't operate in a vacuum—it is tied to habits of holiness and other building blocks we have been considering.

We can give a false impression of appearing to be what we aren't. John says in his epistle about certain people that "they went out from us, but they were not really of us" (1 John 2:19). They were pretenders!

What is inside a person or is being developed there eventually comes out. It may be a quiet and seemingly nice person who becomes a mass murderer. It could also be a Nelson Mandela who walks away from twenty-seven years in prison to become one of our greatest twentieth-century leaders. A Pakistani girl riding home on a school bus is shot in the head by radical Muslims but survives. She becomes the child champion of educational rights for girls with tremendous international influence (see bibliography for her autobiography, *I Am Malala*).

There is an encouraging flip side to this principle. Even though we may have devoted ourselves to habits of holiness in every major area, we may still fail miserably. In the short term, we can be pitifully untrue to who we really are. Suppose a godly husband and father severely compromises his principles for a short time. How should he be counseled? I could see his pastor saying, "Do everything you must to get this behind you. Don't take any shortcuts. Make sure you have someone to whom you are accountable. Keep going! Continue on as the person you really are."

One of the important Christian leaders who helped set the course for my life had an affair with an employee. It was completely out of character with who he was at his core. He quickly did what was necessary to put this behind him, and not only did his marriage survive but he went on to another forty years of leadership in his family, church and other ministries.

Proverbs 24:16 says that "a righteous man falls seven times, and rises again." In *Falling Upward*, Richard Rohr says that his fallings and failings became trampolines to jump higher (12). We don't plan to fall, but must get up and keep going if we do.

Positive long-term change breaks down without habits of holiness becoming ingrained or internalized. Second Corinthians 7:1 exhorts us to "cleanse ourselves from all defilement of flesh and spirit, perfecting holiness in the fear of God." We are considering the idea of "perfecting holiness in the fear of God" over a longer period of time. Without this process, whatever change or growth we experience can be marred or wiped out.

Paul asserts in 1 Corinthians 9:27, "I discipline my body and make it my slave, so that, after I have preached to others, I myself will not be disqualified." Our reputation, positioning for service or leadership can be replaced by shame, guilt, remorse or loss. Paul guarded himself from this fate by practicing physical discipline. We have no choice but to do the same.

Most of us have had some experience in which what we desperately wanted didn't work. We knew what we should do, resist or run away from, but it didn't happen. We failed! Paul says, "I am not practicing what I would like to do, but I am doing the very thing I hate. . . . For the good that I want, I do not do, but I practice the very evil that I do not want. . . . I see a different law in the members of my body, waging war against the law of my mind and making me a prisoner of the law of sin which is in my members" (Romans 7:15, 19, 23).

Romans 8:2 follows this dark and discouraging passage. Yes, "the law of the Spirit of life in Christ Jesus has set you free from the law of sin and of death." Somehow this law doesn't function without our cooperation. We can fly, but we have to get on the airplane.

It is critical that we find our way to habits of holiness. We can't escape Peter's very clear directive, "I urge you as aliens and strangers to abstain from fleshly lusts which wage war against the soul" (1 Peter 2:11). I have said in essence at times, "Lord, I don't want to be tempted by vile thoughts or behaviors. Why don't You remove even the temptations from these things? Why should I be tempted when I am Your child with a new nature?"

The answer is simple. In God's providence and wisdom, we are permitted to have a continuing battle and develop habits of holiness to win the unsavory war we fight. The battle is not removed but resources are provided until at the end we become the people that God intends us to be. Removing the battle and temptations we face would short circuit the plan.

We have embarked on an entire life. Techniques and formulas are good, such as replacing an evil thought with a good one, going to the gym to work out until the temptation passes, or even fasting a day a week to build more discipline into life. These practices and others may be an important part of Christian living, part of the package but not the whole, as the following story illustrates.

James Finley went to the famous monastery, the Abbey of Gethsemane in Kentucky, to practice the disciplines and remove the hindrances to the elevated spiritual life for which he searched. It didn't work. He left the monastery to find the life he couldn't as a monk. Things didn't go well either after he left. Describing this experience in *Christian Meditation: Experiencing the Presence of God; A Guide to Contemplation* (San Francisco: HarperSanFrancisco, 2004), Finley said, "I went kind of crazy for a while, I got drunk a lot, dropped out of church, got depressed, and, to make myself feel better, got married to someone as wounded as I was" (103).

He persevered through his long struggle after leaving the abbey and eventually founded a spiritual life center out west. His formula, "Become a monk and be transformed into a holy man," didn't work. He had to construct a life and become a holy man outside the monastery.

For all of us, building habits of holiness into our lives is one of the ways we are delivered from special or fierce temptation when it comes. First Corinthians 10:13 says, "No temptation has overtaken you but such as is common to man; and God is faithful, who will not allow you to be tempted beyond what you are able, but with the temptation will provide the way of escape also, so that you will be able endure it." Persevering in building Scripture into our lives helps prepare us to win the battles that invariably will come.

Psalm 119:9 directs this idea to youth: "How can a young man keep his way pure? By keeping it according to Your word." Integrating biblical truth into our lives is like practicing for a sport. For example, a basketball player may make 80 percent of his three-point shots at practice, but that's not good enough. "How many can you make during the game" is the real question. For us, the *real game* of living a holy life may occur on the enemy's turf or when we must fend off a brutal attack when we are already in a weakened state.

"Sin which doth so easily beset us" (KJV) or "the sin which so easily entangles us" (Heb. 12:1) isn't removed without our involvement. Getting rid of dark practices and hidden corrupted aspects of our lives is not comfortable or pleasant. Getting fleas off a mangy dog is irritating to his already traumatized hide. There is no easy way, but long-term change is our pathway to victory in areas where we have failed multiple times, month after month or year after year.

Habits of holiness will play a part in the realization of the following prayer: "Now may the God of peace Himself sanctify you entirely; and may your spirit and soul and body be preserved complete, without blame at the coming of our Lord Jesus Christ" (1 Thess. 5:23). Yes! Spirit, soul and body sanctified entirely and preserved complete! Required—developing habits of holiness!

Recently, I recalled a strange conclusion from an Old Testament book of the Bible. It fits. The passage is from the prophet Zechariah: "In that day there will be inscribed on the bells of the horses, 'HOLY TO THE LORD.' And the cooking pots in the LORD's house will be like the bowls before the altar. Every cooking pot in Jerusalem and in Judah will be holy to the LORD of hosts" (Zech. 14:20–21). This means that not only the people but the culture, society, and the accouterments of it will all be holy—holiness penetrating the whole and dispelling anything else. In our hopelessly corrupt environment we are to live holy lives before this is fulfilled during a future millennial era.

For Reflection and Discussion

1. How would you summarize this chapter?
2. With which habits of holiness do you struggle the most?
3. Whatever your current failures might be, what kind of progress have you experienced during the last five years?
4. Which practices are the most helpful in enabling you to live according to the freeing standards given us in the Bible—habits of holiness?

21

The Mind Matters

Reading this chapter should not only drive us to think but also to change something in the way we think. One of our greatest capacities as human beings is the ability to think. Animals have it too but only in the faintest capacity we have. Thinking helps distinguish us as the zenith of God's creation. The tragedy is that 99 percent of those who read this chapter—myself included—abuse, mismanage, and distort this wonderful capacity.

What troubles you most about your thought life? What aspect(s) of your thinking is most difficult to get a handle on? How frequently do your thoughts seem to get out of control?

However you might have answered these questions, the reality is that we think continually. We think good thoughts, bad thoughts, fearful, holy, unholy, inspirational, rational, irrational, despicable, biblical, occasionally heretical, nonsensical, heroic, cowardly, creative, monumental or just routine thoughts. In whatever ways, patterns or habits, we think day and night and in between. We think when we don't want to. We try to control our thoughts and often we can't. We are thinking, reasoning, thought-directed beings.

Yet we seldom think how much our thoughts determine the way we live. Can we pray without using our minds? Or use the Bible? Choose sin or holiness? Love God? (We are to love Him with heart, soul and *mind!*) Making choices? Loving others? (Love must be shaped by knowledge and judgment, which are functions of the mind—Philippians 1:9)

A vast amount of material relating to the use of the mind is included in the Bible along with a large vocabulary of words for the thinking process. Proverbs 23:7 observes that *as we think in our hearts, so are we.* The way we think determines the way we exist in the world. We are familiar with René Descartes's pronouncement, "I think, therefore I am." The ability to think is fundamental to our identity, existence, and personhood as humans. It is not strange that the way we use our minds is critical to the long-term change we seek as Christians.

The Bible in various places affirms the human mind's capacity for thought and reason. Colossians 3:2 indicates that our reasoned choices determine our life orientation. In Romans 14:14, the apostle Paul notes that our minds are basic to the discerning process. Ephesians 3:20 claims that our thinking shapes our expectations and that God can exceed the best of them.

Mary's reaction (Luke 2:19) to the angelic announcement is a classic example of mental functioning. The momentous news she received from Gabriel, the mighty archangel of God, was too much to absorb or process immediately. She pondered, reflected and stored up the stunning information to gain clearer understanding with the passage of time. We too will never understand fully the amazing realms of truth and reality which belong to us. Using our mental facilities, we store up what we can, reflect, wrestle and gain progressive insights.

The essential process of meditation which opens up the treasures of the Bible is a function of the mind (see chap. 17). Paul assures Timothy that his progress will become obvious to others when he disciplines his mind in this way (1 Tim. 4:15). He elevates the idea further in 2 Timothy 2:15, assuring his protégé that the mental process of studying Scripture wisely will result in approval from the *audience of One*: "Be diligent to present yourself approved to God as a workman who does not need to be ashamed, accurately handling the word of truth."

In his exposition of Jesus' teaching in Matthew 5:29–30 about taking radical action to discipline ourselves in dealing with sin, Oswald Chambers put it this way: "'The good is the enemy of the best . . .' in every man, the bad never is, but the good that is not good enough" (*Studies in the Sermon on the Mount*, 4th ed. [London: Simpkin, Marshall, 1929], 22). Similarly, Paul prays for the Philippian Christians that they will choose between many options (including what is good and desirable) and come out with excellent choices that will exceed the options they reject (Phil. 1:9–11). Using the mind as a controller will keep us steady when faced with powerful forces that may or may not lead us in the right direction. Paul underscores this conclusion when he says that he would prefer to speak only five words guided by reasoned understanding than ten thousand in an unknown tongue (1 Cor. 14:19).

To focus more clearly on how the mind affects long-term change in our Christian experience, two verses give critical insights. The first focuses on the process demanded of us. Romans 12:2 gives us two remarkably different directives: "Do not be conformed to this world, but be transformed by the renewing of your mind, so that you may prove what the will of God is, that which is good and acceptable and perfect."

The first directive warns against conformity to the world. The verb in Greek relates to the word *schematic*. If we channel electrical current through a schematic such as the wiring of a washing machine, dishwasher, toaster, digital movie projector, or any number of other pieces of equipment, that's a positive way to control power. But when we permit our lives to be controlled by the "currents" of the world and contemporary culture, we can properly be called *worldlings* and are guaranteed a failed life.

The second controlling principle is our only reasonable course of action: *transformation*. The mind drives the process of change according to Romans 12:2. We are to be *transformed by the renewing of our minds*. This word is transferred directly to English as metamorphosis. It is exemplified by the transformation of a pupa into a gorgeous butterfly. The transformation is programmed into the organism. Cut into the cocoon to help the process and it is destroyed.

We store life-changing material into our minds, biblical truths basic to the Christian life. This drives the process of transformed thinking for a transformed life. This high-level, exalted living occurs when we are compelled from within. The mind is highlighted as the controller of the process in Romans 12:2. Long-term change is impossible without ongoing transformation being directed by the mind!

Philippians 4:8 describes how this is to work out. "Whatever is true, whatever is honorable, whatever is right, whatever is pure, whatever is lovely, whatever is of good repute, if there is any excellence and if anything worthy of praise, dwell [or *think*] on these things." It is a radical idea that an eightfold grid is the filter through which our thoughts should pass:

The Mind Matters

- true
- honorable
- right
- pure
- lovely
- good repute (reputation)
- excellent
- worthy of praise

This is like trying to pole vault twenty-five feet—you jump as high as you can and are the better for it even if you never reach twenty-five feet.

What is programmed into our thinking becomes reality in our lives and the standards set in this verse become an invitation to long-term change. If it's true that to a large extent we are what we think, it works both ways, either for good or for ill. As the saying goes, "Sow a thought, reap an action; sow an action, reap a habit; sow a habit, reap a character; sow a character, reap a destiny."

At the beginning of the year it became obvious that I must address an unhealthy syndrome in my thought life. The more I monitored my thinking, I observed that it was even worse than I thought. I used the acronym of NARB to describe my syndrome and get a handle on my destructive thought patterns immediately when I was falling into them. I felt like a prisoner in the four walls of this NARB pattern. A jail break would not be easy. The cell was well constructed.

Here is my prison cell with the name plate, NARB:

> *N* represents *negative*, counterproductive patterns that are woven into the way I think. For example, I sometimes waste energy disliking a TV star or other public

personality and figure out ways to down them in my mind. A web of negative thinking so easily pervades my thought life.

A is for *anger* I experience over frustrating, annoying details that I can't prevent. For years, losing my temper occasionally was a fact of my life. I could be angry for an hour after another driver did something inconsiderate or dangerous. My occasions to be angry were many—I could find something to be angry about almost every day from the newspaper.

R equals *resentment!* I felt hostility toward prominent people who appeared to be unworthy, undeserving, and incompetent, yet flaunted themselves in their roles. Since I had wanted to be a prominent pastor and speaker, I often resented pastors I heard or speakers on the radio.

B is for the *bitterness* that poisoned my thinking. It is linked to and not always distinguishable from resentment. It may be a little more disguised. It always seemed to be lurking beneath the surface of my emotions or mind and was easily triggered. It was rooted in unhealed wounds related to what I failed to accomplish or was denied.

I discovered that I had to add an *S* to make NARBS. *S* identified my pattern of *stewing* over my NARB elements. Negative, angry, resentful and bitter thoughts could occupy my mind for hours. As I became more sensitive to this counterproductive spiral which not only wasted time but further ingrained my NARB patterns, I began to identify and get rid of these counterproductive thoughts and substitute them with things I could give thanks or pray for in a positive manner.

Just getting a mental click on NARBS when I began to descend into my old patterns was helpful. I sensed greater freedom—like opening a window to let in fresh air. Even though this requires making uncomfortable choices, this new way of thinking is liberating me from the old, condemned patterns. The changes are exhilarating even though I am finding it hard sometimes to turn my back on old reactions.

Transformation or long-term change directed by the mind is pictured in a verse I memorized years ago. In 2 Corinthians 10:5 we see the idea of bringing each thought into captivity or alignment to a life with Christ: "We are destroying speculations and every lofty thing raised up against the knowledge of God, and are taking *every thought captive* to the obedience of Christ." Every thought! A great target! With me now, I believe it is safe to say, *in process . . . with progress* to sum up how things are going.

How could we fail to be challenged by reading this chapter seriously? Perhaps each of us should refuse to leave it until we have been driven to make some change in our thinking. Read it over again. Highlight what stands out to you. Review passages on the mind until you have expanded the way you think about thinking. Choose what you will attempt to implement. The mind is an amazing asset and capacity and must be harnessed and directed for us to become who and what we should be. This chapter has given us a call and opportunity to be serious about this process for the rest of our lives.

For Reflection and Discussion
1. Have you taken care to protect how you think?
2. Where are you vulnerable in your thought life?
3. What further changes must you make?

4. This follow-up or review project will help you pull together what we considered in this chapter. Philippians 4:8 catalogues the components of desirable thinking. List these elements and attempt to use them to bracket the way the way you think.

22

Suffering and Affliction

Building Blocks Nobody Wants

Have you discovered that people you would least expect have heartbreak, suffering, or pain in their lives? Unless you're unusually perceptive, you *won't see their hidden hurts.* We live with brokenness, have "demon" issues that haunt us, live with profound hurts, and confront problems we can't handle.

Richard Rohr writes as one who knows by experience from more than forty years of working with such people:

> There is a strange and even wonderful communion in real human pain, actually much more than in joy, which is too often manufactured and passing. In one sense, pain's effects are not passing. . . .
>
> The genius of the Gospel is that it included the problem inside the solution. The falling became the standing. The stumbling became the finding. The dying became the rising. The raft became the shore. The small self cannot see this very easily, because it . . . is still too fragile, and

is caught up in the tragedy of it all. It has not lived long enough to see the big patterns. (*Falling Upward*, vii, 158–59)

I recall the substance of a theologian's comment that he didn't learn a great deal from the blessings that had been poured out on him, but he profited profoundly from what he had suffered. None of us want the sufferings and afflictions that come into our lives. However, they become the furnace in which we are refined. Psalm 66:10 says, "You have tried us, O God; You have refined us as silver is refined." This is great theoretically, but it can be brutal to experience.

Our faith moves us beyond fatalism, apparent purposelessness in our suffering, or bitterness. The apostle Peter says, "After you have suffered for a little while, the God of all grace, who called you to His eternal glory in Christ, will Himself perfect, confirm, strengthen and establish you" (1 Peter 5:10). This is the common *modus operandi* for the majority of Christians who live deeply with God. They have paid the price to punch their ticket to a spiritual life which runs deeply beneath the surface.

You don't ask for it, court it or try to find it. Suffering and affliction will find you, even as God is with you in it. Suffering and affliction are unwanted ingredients of long-term change. Rohr claims, "There always will be at least one situation in our lives that we cannot fix, control, explain, change, or even understand" (Rohr, *Falling Upward*, 68).

A series of monographs by T. S. Rendall compiled as *In God's School: Scriptural Studies Dealing with Various Disciplines Employed by God in the Training of His Children* (Three Hills, AB, Canada: Prairie Press, 1971), grouped afflictive experiences that Christians endure under *D*s. Each was titled "God's Discipline of. . . ." His *D* labels for the suffering and affliction we commonly endure are darkness, disturbance, detour, delay, disappointment, distress, denial, dilemma, determent, and defeat. Raymond Edman offers his list of thirty *D*s in his book *The Disciplines of Life* ([Eugene, OR: Harvest House Publishers, 1982], 4–5). In his table of contents he lists each as "The Discipline of . . ." declining days, danger, defamation, deformity, desolation, desperation, disability, disillusionment, doubt, durability, and others.

Do any of these cause sadness, pain remembered or lingering heartbreak from past experiences? More than one triggers painful memories from circumstances I experienced. Yet they also bring a certain reverence of having walked through with God's eventual intervention. The apostle Peter encourages those who are receiving his epistle "that the same experiences of suffering are being accomplished by your brethren who are in the world" (1 Peter 5:9). It would be almost impossible to go through your Christian life without having to cope with one of these conditions. He says further, "To the degree that you share the sufferings of Christ, keep on rejoicing" (4:13). Paul too speaks of the "fellowship of His sufferings" in Philippians 3:10. People aren't standing in line to gain entrance into this elite club, but what we endure becomes the entry fee.

The psalmist pounds this theme of affliction like a bass drum in Psalm 119. He affirms the benefits and we can hear his words reverently whether tears are still wet on our cheeks or are we looking back. "Look upon my affliction and rescue me. . . . This is my comfort in my affliction, that Your word has revived me. . . . Before I was afflicted I went astray, but now I keep Your word. . . . It is good for me that I was afflicted, that I may learn Your statutes. . . . I am exceedingly afflicted; revive me, O Lord, according to Your word" (vv. 153, 50, 67, 71, 107). It is difficult to read these verses without identifying with his experience.

I remember a statement from Charles Ryrie in a class he taught. It is the simple yet profound truth that God uses *means*. He uses the *means* of what afflicts us or causes suffering as a wise Father for His very high ends. "What son is there whom his father does not discipline? But if you are without discipline, of which all have become partakers, then you are illegitimate children and not sons. . . . Shall we not much rather be subject to the Father of spirits, and live? . . . He disciplines us for our good, so that we may share His holiness" (Heb. 12:7–10).

To sharpen the point of this chapter, we can review some of the results that our sufferings or afflictions bring. First Peter 4:1 is dramatic like a gun blast in its finality. Once the bullet leaves the barrel, you can't call it back. We can't dodge this bullet. The idea of being armed (like carrying a gun) is right in the verse! The rifle shot is like this: Do you want to cease from sin? Suffer! The trigger is pulled and the ammo (suffering) fired. Peter says, "Therefore, since Christ has suffered in the flesh, arm yourselves also with the same purpose, because he who has suffered in the flesh has ceased from sin."

This Petrine epistle is about suffering. The apostle pretty much says it like Forrest Gump: "And that's all I have to say about that." If you want to be able to overcome sin, suffer! If you wish to go beyond the starkness of Peter's pronouncement, go to other passages that give a little more context to this painful topic. For example, Hebrews 12:4–11 explains that we develop holiness and righteousness through suffering under God our Father's loving discipline. Psalm 119:67 notes how our afflictions can keep us from straying. Romans 5:3–4 teaches that tribulations develop our ability to persevere. Referring again to 1 Peter 5, our trials lead to the tremendous results of being perfected, confirmed, strengthened, and established. Verses 50 and 71 of Psalm 119 emphasize that we are driven to experience the power of Scripture beyond what we do in pleasant times of life. No wonder the author of Hebrews says we are to "buck up," endure them all, and come out on the other side (Heb. 12:12–13). Maybe 1 Peter 4:1 makes more sense when surrounded by all the positives we've noted here.

Hard times, afflictions or sufferings have their part in the long journey in which we change and grow up as we should. However, in this next chapter, we are led to a higher threshold through even deeper darkness and crisis than we considered in this chapter. Contemplatives call it *the dark night of the soul*. I wrote about it with fear and trembling in the book entitled *An Evangelical's Road Less Traveled: A Contemplative Life*.

For Reflection and Discussion

1. Do you find the theme of this chapter something you would rather not consider now? If so, why?
2. Can you think of one benefit you have already received from what you have endured?
3. To keep you grounded, why not choose two or three biblical passages we considered in this chapter or elsewhere in the Bible and study them until you have gained the familiarity you may need.
4. Take a few moments to pray or be with God as a final exercise after considering this hard subject.

23

Crisis Transformation

Do you live with a sense of dread about some terrible thing that might happen? Horrendous crises can barge into our lives without notice. They level the playing field of humanity whether we are at the bottom or top or in between. They create circumstances that can change our lives forever.

Such was the case with Michael, a CFO, retired in his forties with a platinum parachute when his billion-dollar firm was sold. His active, athletic wife ran marathons and climbed mountains. We had picnicked together in the majestic Big Snowy Mountains in central Montana on the way to their summer home. She pointed out a mountain she climbed as we munched our lunch.

He called me one day with an urgent prayer request: "Sherry has been diagnosed with cancer that has metastasized in her lymph nodes." Ever got a call like that? What do you say? There are no easy answers, but there are principles that help shine light during times of such impenetrable darkness.

Jacob in the book of Genesis can help us explore this type of dark chasm in our lives. It is repeated in every generation of God's people. We can compare this strange and mysterious occurrence to what happens in a blacksmith shop. (This topic is treated in some detail in the chapter titled "Peniel—Crisis Transformation" in *Beyond Leadership to Destiny*, listed in the front of this book.) A blacksmith heats a piece of metal until it is red hot and then strikes an insignificant blow with a small hammer. This place marks the spot where the heavy sledge will smash the metal to mold it to its final shape. God had brought Jacob to Bethel and marked his life for years of formation. He had been in the fire for twenty years and said as much (Gen. 31:40–41). Now he was on the anvil to receive the "molding blow" in which he would be permanently injured, limping away with a new name and ultimately a new identity.

Jacob's crushing experience along the banks of the Jabbok River came because he thought his brother Esau was coming to eradicate him, his large family and huge retinue of servants and cattle. He had become a wealthy man in his exile and now Esau and his band of four hundred desert warriors could destroy everything. You can read this episode in Genesis 32.

His time *alone with the Alone* along the banks of the Jabbok River provided the context which Brother Roger of Taizé describes, "In every one lies a zone of solitude that no human intimacy can fill; and there God encounters us." Even though a company of angels met him just before this incident (Gen. 32:1–2), he needed further preparation for what was about to happen.

The forced solitude and struggle at Peniel can be a model for us. In his book *Invitation to a Journey: A Road Map for Spiritual Formation* (Downers Grove, IL: InterVarsity Press, 1985), Robert Mulholland captures it well:

> This is what solitude is: in the silence of releasing control of our relationship with God to God, coming face to face with the kind of person we are in the depths of our being; seeing the depths of our grasping manipulative, self-indulgent behavior; facing the brokenness, the darkness, the uncleanness that is within; acknowledging our bondages, our false securities, our posturing facades; and naming ourselves to God as this kind of person. . . . In silence we let go our manipulative control. In solitude we face up to what we are in the depths of our being. Prayer then becomes the offering of who we are to God: the giving of that broken, unclean, grasping, manipulative self to God for the work of God's grace in our lives. (140)

At Peniel we face ourselves. We hear our name. We confess who we are, no matter how bad it looks and feels. The awesome reality is that God enters into our broken lives to identify what He sees us to be (2 Cor. 5:17). His pronouncement assures the result. When He says, "It is Israel, Prince with God" (instead of Jacob, the heel grabber), then Israel it really is. There is a sense in which when we endure deep crises and the transformation that results, we too gain a new dimension of life with some level of changed identity and persona.

From Jacob's time until now, God's people have spent time in circumstances that could be likened to a "torture track" while select chapters of their lives are being written. I am reminded of a time when I drove tractors that were being tested to the extreme before they were put into production.

I spent one shift on the torture track. While I was test-driving tractors, the order finally came, "You're on the torture track tonight." The tractor I was assigned had more than four thousand pounds of extra weight attached to the front axle (equivalent to two compact cars) and had to be driven over large ridges with speed bumps for the entire shift. I jammed my feet across the windshield crossbar to prevent back injury and was thrown into the ceiling. Nothing helped. Months of testing were compressed into hours on the torture track to get a production model tractor for use around the world.

Soon after my shift on the torture track, it began to be called the "Nebraska Strip." Stoic men were excited. Tests which destroyed equipment and punished the people who drove them were finished. One of our tractors was being shipped to Nebraska to become a production model for use around the world.

That's what happened to Jacob at Peniel—he became a production model. He spent twenty years on the *test track* with Uncle Laban and endured a stint on the *torture track* at Peniel. At sunrise the next day he limped out with his model designation, *Prince with God*. So that's what God is doing at our Peniels as well—making us production models to stand the test of time and *beyond*. Just as Kenneth Caraway once wrote, "There is no box made by God nor by us but that the sides can be flattened out and the top blown off to make a dance floor on which to celebrate life" ("Boxed In, But Not Out," *Alive Now!* [March/April 1974]: 15). Our extreme and dark experiences which appear to be hopeless can likewise end in celebration! We probably don't realize how this could happen, but God does!

Peniel is not primarily a package but a principle. Jacob's encounter at what became Peniel was limited to a few square yards along a small river flowing from the eastern frontier in Gilead to the Jordan. Time limitations made it an experience of twelve hours or less (Gen. 32:22, 24).

Your Peniel may extend halfway around the world through burning days and anguished months. The predetermined end is the same. *In the darkness of a major life crisis, a permanent forward step is taken in God's foundational plan for your life.* He uses an arena of focused interests, drives, or motivations to lead you to wrestle from Him the blessing of a lifetime. In some great suffocating experience, what is so twisted into the fabric of a life structure without any possibility of being changed *can be changed*! This is the Peniel Principle!

Perhaps the whole book of Job is a biographical case in point. Job had achieved a spiritual state which was unexcelled in the world in his time and proved to be the one candidate to qualify for the grim task of having everything stripped away. After being wealthy, influential, and blessed with a large family, it was all taken away so that he sat desolate and mocked scraping his body with a piece of broken pottery at the local ash dump.

However, as writers who explore crisis transformation point out, Job had not yet reached the place where he must go according to God's plan for his life. In *Mysticism: A Study in the Nature and Development of Spiritual Consciousness* (1930; repr., Mineola, NY: Dover Publications, 2002), Evelyn Underhill captured it like this:

> [This] apparently selfless state, the 'I, the Me, the Mine,' though spiritualized, still remained intact . . . [William Law says,] "But still, in all this show and glitter of virtue, there is an unpurified bottom on which they stand, there is a selfishness which can no more enter into the Kingdom of Heaven than the grossness of flesh and blood can enter into it. . . ."
>
> The self, then, has got to learn to cease to be its "own centre and circumference": to make that final surrender

> which is the price of final peace. In the Dark Night the starved and tortured spirit learns through an anguish . . . to accept lovelessness for the sake of Love, Nothingness for the sake of the All; dies without any sure promise of life, loses when it hardly hopes to find. It sees with amazement the most sure foundations of its transcendental life crumble beneath it, dwells in a darkness which seems to hold no promise of a dawn . . . the last test of heroic detachment, of manliness, of spiritual courage. (396–97)

Jacob likewise was to experience a transformative action of God which elevated his life in a type of resurrection from his death-like circumstance. Jacob descended into pure darkness at the prospect of his entire family being wiped out and losing everything meaningful to him. He was permanently wounded never to walk normally again. Yet the account ends with Jacob becoming Israel (Prince with God) with a level of light and life with God that places him among the great saints of the ages.

John 12:24 encapsulates the dark-night stage of crisis transformation. "Truly, truly, I say to you, unless a grain of wheat falls into the earth and dies, it remains alone; but if it dies, it bears much fruit." This verse and the idea of crisis transformation are explored further in my book *Dying to Live*.

The apostle Paul in 2 Corinthians 1:8–9 speaks about a dying-to-living episode in his own life: "For we do not want you to be unaware, brethren, of our affliction which came to us in Asia, that we were burdened excessively, beyond our strength, so that we despaired even of life; indeed, we had the sentence of death within ourselves so that we would not trust in ourselves, but in God who raises the dead."

It took this circumstance in the apostle's life during his journey through Asia Minor to Philippi to take him beyond his own capacities to despair. It was through this death-like experience, he received a transformative action of God which elevated his life in a type of resurrection or new level of life.

Long-term change! Like it or not, you may be inducted into this elite spiritual condition as thousands have before you by means of what appears to be a terrible experience. Apparently, by a special action of God we get plugged into a resurrection quality of life that is impossible before it happens.

I don't think we punch our own ticket or call our own shots for this level of long-term change through crisis transformation. However it takes place, God brings the result to pass in the darkest of circumstances to bring us to a level of living we have never known before.

For Reflection and Discussion

1. What is your immediate emotional reaction to this chapter?
2. Would you wish to avoid a crisis transformation experience at any cost and stay at a high-level spiritual state without it?
3. How would you describe *crisis transformation* as we have addressed it in this chapter? Do you accept this as a valid concept of the spiritual life?
4. Would you discuss this with a fellow believer or is it too dark a theme?

24

Healing

What Is Holding Us Back?

We can be and often are broken in numerous ways and places. Being a Christian does not necessarily mean that we are no longer affected by wounds, scars, deficiencies, or flawed elements of our lives. The purpose of this chapter is *not* to explore the huge subject of our ills and deformities as a therapist might. Thousands of Christian counselors and shelves of books offer an integration of biblical principles with counseling practices.

The purpose of this chapter *is to call attention to the need for healing in areas which thwart long-term change.* David Seamands was a pioneer in developing a counseling approach directed to Christians which included an integration of biblical principles into treatment practices. His case for this inner healing is compelling.

In his book *Healing for Damaged Emotions* (Wheaton: Victor Books: 1981), Seamands claims that like the rings of a tree which record the conditions in which a tree grew,

[i]n the rings of our thoughts and emotions, the record is there; the memories are recorded, and all are alive. And they directly and deeply affect our concepts, our feelings, and our relationships. They affect the way we look at life and God, at others and ourselves. . . . [S]alvation does not give instant emotional health . . . . [C]ertain areas of our lives need special healing by the Holy Spirit. Because they are not subject to ordinary prayer, discipline, and willpower, they need a special kind of understanding, an unlearning of past wrong programming, and a relearning and reprogramming transformation by the renewal of our minds. And this is not done overnight . . . ." (12–13)

Many of us have areas of woundedness, deformity, brokenness or darkness that need to be treated as we continue our journey toward long-term change. A word of caution: There are appropriate times and seasons in our lives. Some people may not be ready to address life issues that hold them prisoner. Others may need to share this phase of their journey with a professional counselor. Proceed if you are ready, but feel free to pass over this chapter if you need to.

A nationally known business leader shocked me with his response to a query about his major concerns as he began the Life Serve mentoring program. His major concern—woundedness! A mature Christian woman and serious student of Scripture, when discussing an explosive area in her life, said, "I'm stuck." She had outstanding personal, spiritual and emotional resources to address this issue, but she remained *stuck*. This chapter is a call toward healing and restoration for those who are *stuck*. For some, living with deficiency, darkness or deformed elements of life has become so normal that they would feel insecure without it. It is so much a part of their lives, that they are dependent on it. I saw a T-shirt with the message, "I like my bad a—— attitude." Apparently, this individual felt better about himself when he could have more control of his life by abusing others with his behavior.

Ephesians 5:27 claims that the day is coming when we will not have any remaining ugly blotches. We will not be able to take our deformities into heaven even if we want to. Now is the time to anticipate what will be the norm then, due to the perfecting work of Christ on our behalf.

The Life Serve segment on healing and restoration claims that "a first step leading to changes we desire is an honest inventory." The check-off list to stimulate this penetrating look within is as follows: "Self-control, strained relationships, eating habits, fear, lust, hatred or bitterness, inability to forgive, guilt or shame, addictions, insecurity, inferiority, failure, depression or discouragement, lack of purpose or meaning, greed, inability to maintain relationships, a persistent feeling that something is not right, or your particular issues" ("Healing and Restoration," in *Life Serve Mentoring Program*, session 1, p. 2).

Pains carried from childhood plague many of us in our adult years. I am surprised, for example, at how frequently relationships with fathers emerge spontaneously when a group of men come together. Where do you feel the greatest need for healing and restoration or wholeness? Do you have the freedom to honestly recognize and admit this area(s) to yourself? What would you most like to have *fixed* in your life? Have you ever brought any of these concerns to the attention of another person for support, prayer or counsel? Have you experienced any breakthroughs with respect to the areas of your life that trouble you?

Asking questions and raising issues in this chapter highlight our need for healing and restoration to the wholeness that is possible for us as part of the long-term change process. Many of us have elements of our lives we have not been able to change. Others have dark areas they have hidden from others. We may feel ashamed, defeated or frustrated on a daily basis.

We are to be encouraged even as we battle these ongoing deficiencies. I have been inspired for a long time with this verse, "The LORD will accomplish [perfect, KJV] what concerns me" (Ps. 138:8). Our final state as the bride of Christ is one of perfection without the blemishes we carry with us now. Even though the process may be difficult, frightening or painful, we can open heart, life and intentions to the healing and restoration that is part of the long-term change process.

For Reflection and Discussion

1. How are you reacting to this chapter? Are you saying, "This subject doesn't concern me?" Do you feel threatened or invaded? Did it make you angry, or did it cause you to look a little more deeply at your life than you normally do?
2. If you uncovered or were reminded of one or more troubling issues in your life, were you able to take an honest look at this concern?
3. Do you feel it might be best to let past issues stay in the past and concentrate on positive growth steps? If so, why?
4. If you come away from this chapter on healing and restoration with something you want to face, do you have an action step to get you started?

Part 4

How the Future Impacts Our Present

One of the basic elements of musical composition is the chord. Without chords, music lacks harmony. In this final section of the book, we are playing one of the resounding chords of the Bible—the future!

Chords have a minimum of three notes and are built off a single note called *the root*. The root note in this section is *the future*. The notes in a chord are played simultaneously. The two supporting notes which make up our chord are the kingdom of God and the second coming of Christ. The three notes combined in our chord say simply that a future perspective is critical to Christian experience.

Like a magnet that orders metal filings around it, so our future focus helps align the elements of our present journey. Abraham is a classic example.

Hebrews 11:8–11 puts a frame around his life to illustrate how the future impacts our present. "By faith Abraham, when he was called, obeyed . . . and he went out, not knowing where he was going. By faith he lived as an alien . . . for he was looking for the city which has foundations, whose architect and builder is God." It makes such good sense! If Abraham was to inherit a city whose Designer and Builder was God Himself, it was all right to be an alien for a while. After all, the best cities that ancient Canaan had to offer were mediocre compared to that.

Saints in any generation and in every conceivable way have been tempted to forfeit an astounding future for a third-rate present. If we are gripped by a reality which we can't see but is very real to us, we will be driven to live lives that are worthy of it. Living *kingdom-worthy lives* will be our vision and only realistic option.

A TV ad speaks to the point. A professor is with a group of people who are trying to determine how much money it will take to finance their retirement years. They were instructed to take ribbon and stretch it out from a center to a peripheral place that would indicate their life expectancy.

Ribbons were stretched all the way out to 105 years! They would be candidates for former weatherman and birthday greeter Willard Scott's Smucker's jellies ads. Two deficiencies stood out. The first is obvious and actuarial scientists are employed to address this issue. Using the data available, they estimate how long people might live. This helps insurance companies and other institutions set their rates. But none of us know how long *we* will live.

The second and more important concern is what happens after a life span that reaches 105 years or less. "Death" is what happens! In the TV ad, the closest reference to death is "life expectancy," without a word about what will occur after one's life has run its course.

In this final segment of the book, we focus on what happens after this life is done and how this future reality helps determine how well we push on to the best result we can achieve in the time span available to us.

First Corinthians 15 is one of the longer chapters in the New Testament. *Death* is mentioned throughout, but so is *resurrection*. There is no avoidance of the reality of death. *Death* and *resurrection* can't be separated for the Christian.

Even so, you may not have heard many sermons or given much attention yourself to the kingdom as treated in the Bible. Likewise, you may not have given serious thought to the second coming of Christ. Since there are different views connected to this future coming, preachers may avoid it as well.

The kingdom of God will involve the direct divine rule of God. In the Lord's Prayer we are instructed to pray for this kingdom: "Our Father who is in heaven . . . Your kingdom come. Your will be done, on earth as it is in heaven" (Matt. 6:9–10).

This coming kingdom means that God will cause His will to be done on earth as it is in heaven. There will no longer be a tragic divide between God's rule in heaven and any number of competing ungodly or even satanic mini-kingdoms in the world. Theologians have written thousands of pages on this coming kingdom, its stages and manifestations. Our baseline consideration claims that there is a future day when God will rule directly and divinely over a creation finally subject to Him.

A verb used by the apostle Paul in Philippians 3:13 has the idea in the Greek of stretching out the neck: "Brethren, I do not regard myself as having laid hold of it yet; but one thing I do: forgetting what lies behind and *reaching forward* to what lies ahead." Paul is like the runner who lunges and stretches toward the finish line. It should be said of us as well that we are "stretching out the neck" in eager anticipation of this coming kingdom. Likewise, we are "looking for the blessed hope and the appearing of the glory of our great God and Savior, Christ Jesus" (Titus 2:13). A final touch is given in seldom-used verses that speak of "those who are Christ's at His coming, then comes the end, when He hands over the kingdom to the God and Father, when He has abolished all rule and all authority and power. For He must reign until He has put all His enemies under His feet" (1 Cor. 15:23–25). We are looking eagerly for this future reality even though it is well hidden now.

We are focusing on kingdom considerations and His second coming as components of long-term change for the believer. We will discover that a biblical emphasis relates them inextricably to growth and development while we live.

25

Kingdom Hope

One commodity seems to be in short supply these days among Christians and other thoughtful people. It is hope for our nation. People struggle with questions such as,

> Where do we go from here?
> Is there much hope for great leaders to emerge today as they did in the past?
> Could such leaders be elected and unify a very divided culture?
> Are we moving toward the end of one of the greatest runs of any nation in the history of the world?
> If we are sliding off the back side of the mountain, is there any realistic hope of getting back to the top?
> Historians have said that great nations last an average of 250 to 300 years. What hope do we have, if any, of increasing that number?

With divorce rates somewhere around 50 percent and so many children being raised without two parents in their home, is there any hope for a healthy generation of young people to follow? Similar divorce rates plague second and third marriages as well. Can a nation that has turned from *the faith of our fathers* and is lost in its own waywardness escape judgment?

As we look at our own nation and consider historical parallels in the past, thinking people often hesitate to speak about the depth of their concerns. Peggy Noonan wrote about this state of mind as related to how we experience time, and after the terrorist attacks of 9/11 she was asked to repost the essay: "Something's up. And deep down, where the body meets the soul, we are fearful. We fear, down so deep it hasn't even risen to the point of articulation, that with all our comforts and amusements, with all our toys and bells and whistles . . . we wonder if what we really have is . . . a first-class stateroom on the *Titanic*. Everything's wonderful, but a world is ending and we sense it" ("There Is No Time, There Will Be Time," *Forbes ASAP*, November 30, 1998, reposted September 18, 2001 by *The Wall Street Journal*, http://online.wsj.com/news/articles/SB122409083174236943). Noonan is not alone in her observation. Other prophetic voices, secular and religious, echo the same message.

Could it be counterintuitive but correct to say that the decline of our nation has potential benefit for us as Christians? Can we be shoved in the right direction by the specter of the potential future demise of our nation? Do we need to separate more thoroughly our anticipation of God's kingdom from attachment to our own nation?

I remember a Bible teacher using the illustration of workmen sanding down and painting the rails of the *Titanic* before it hit the iceberg if we make our focus the saving of our country from destruction. Are we sanding the rails of the *Titanic* when we dedicate our energy to saving our country from self-destructing?

Hope in a hopeless world is a great theme of the Bible. Hope as described in Scripture drives long-term change. Romans 5:5 claims that hope will not leave us ashamed. Hitler held out hope for a discouraged nation of Germans. So did Lenin and Stalin in Russia. Today they are dark memories. These leaders who at one time espoused hope left a legacy of shame, revulsion, disgrace and hopelessness. Our current president chose hope as a campaign theme. Some people have lost the hope they had when he was elected. In fact, the Bible makes the point that any temporal expectation can leave us empty and without hope. Sometimes we are slow as believers to hope for what God has put in front of us, instead of what we see all around and cling to.

Hope in God's kingdom which goes beyond anything we can experience now reverberates in both Old and New Testaments. This *kingdom hope* has a role in driving us to long-term change. It helps determine what we are expecting and moving toward. Olympic athletes toil for years to procure a medal which they will acquire or lose in a few moments of competition. Paul uses this analogy to point out the need to turn away from the corruptible to the incorruptible in terms of the prize we are seeking (1 Cor. 9:25).

We have a bewildering array of references that lead us to *kingdom hope* in the Bible. Seeking His kingdom promises eventual and complete provision, according to Matthew 6:33.

The reality of God's kingdom drives us to lives inscribed with righteousness, peace and joy, according to Romans 14:17. These priceless commodities are pursued, developed and experienced over time when our focus goes beyond the temporal.

Demas fell away from this reality and the apostle describes him as "having loved this present world" (2 Tim. 4:10 KJV). His hope of a coming kingdom was what he was holding onto in his present world. In so doing, he becomes the antithesis of what we are considering.

Abraham was willing to turn his back on all other options to gain a city "whose builder and maker is God" (Heb. 11:10 KJV). The beatitudes in Matthew 5 are all about apparent losers in life who are incredibly blessed as kingdom participants. "Blessed are the poor in spirit, for theirs is the kingdom of heaven" (Matt. 5:3).

References and instruction about the hope we have as members of the kingdom of God could be included by the dozens. There are more than 150 references to the kingdom in the New Testament alone. Our focus here is to connect us with the truth that long-term change involves being steadfast in the hope we have as participants in this kingdom.

Paul claims in 1 Thessalonians 2:12 that it is essential "that you would walk in a manner worthy of the God who calls you into His own kingdom and glory." We are way up the mountain slope in this verse. We are people on whom the call of God rests. The summit is the kingdom of God and the glory of it! We are not to be mucking about in the swamps, as an Englishman might say.

Having our feet planted firmly in kingdom realities will help us pursue long-term change and continue to invest ourselves in what is valuable to God throughout the course of our lives. "Since we receive a kingdom which cannot be shaken, let us show gratitude, by which we may offer to God an acceptable service with reverence and awe" (Heb. 12:28). We have every reason to persevere over a lifetime to get as far as we can in loving, serving and growing up as kingdom people.

For Reflection and Discussion

1. What do you understand the kingdom of God to be or how would you define it?
2. How meaningful is it for you to be a part of it?
3. How does being a part of God's kingdom affect the way you are living?
4. Have you ever taken time to examine what the Bible says about *the kingdom of God*? (If not, consider putting a kingdom study on your project list.)

26

Anticipating the Coming

We are considering how future hope for the believer contributes to long-term change. A fixed hope in God's kingdom to come was critical in the life of Abraham and other Old Testament saints. We ramp up another notch when we look at what the New Testament says about the coming of Christ for Christians.

A pitch-dark contrast is the phenomenon of the numerous suicides by celebrities. A bizarre suicide attempt by a rapper who uses the name "Christ Bearer" made headlines earlier this year. "Stunned" is the word Steve Martin used in a tweet to express his reaction to news of the suicide of Oscar-winning actor and comedian Robin Williams. While each case has its own history and causes, a stark reality is suggested. When our hope is invested in dreams that go no further than finite circumstances, we can be severely disappointed when we get *there*—whatever *there* is for each of us.

Psychologists have noted that some level of depression often follows after a person reaches the pinnacle of life they sought for a long period of time. An NFL quarterback, as he and his team were winning a Super Bowl, asked late in the game, "Is this all there is to it?"

Being at the top doesn't fill the hole or vacuum in our human hearts. This is the timeless message and verdict of Ecclesiastes. For example, Moses was "at the top" as an adopted member of the royal family, and yet he turned his back on such privilege. The author of Hebrews makes the mysterious statement that *the reproach of Christ* drove him beyond the royal treasure-filled life he enjoyed in Egypt. Hebrews 11:24–26 notes that "by faith Moses, when he had grown up, refused to be called the son of Pharaoh's daughter, choosing rather to endure ill-treatment with the people of God than to enjoy the passing pleasures of sin, considering the *reproach of Christ* greater riches than the treasures of Egypt; for he was looking to the reward."

As New Testament believers, we have a much clearer idea of kingdom realities. We noted Hebrews 12:28 in the previous chapter: "Since we receive a kingdom which cannot be shaken, let us show gratitude, by which we may offer to God an acceptable service with reverence and awe." Old Testament saints grasped this reality with the limited knowledge they had. We have a much fuller revelation on which to grab hold and continue on in the face of every obstacle we must face.

Abraham or Moses didn't have the incredible statement from the Lord given first in Isaiah 64:4 and then quoted for us by Paul in 1 Corinthians 2:9: "Things which the eye has not seen and ear has not heard, and which have not entered the heart of man, all that God has prepared for those who love Him." We don't have categories, capabilities or conceptual abilities to take in what will be ours.

Ephesians 2:7 says "that in the ages to come He might show the surpassing riches of His grace in kindness toward us in Christ Jesus." As I am struggling these days to meet some of the challenges that are coming my way, I have been anchored by this verse. It's the idea, "Charles, what you are experiencing and facing isn't going to last forever. Persevere until you get to your incredible future, which will make your current pain and heartache become momentary in comparison."

The apostle John underscores this rigorous demand of persevering now to gain what is to come when he writes from his exile home off the coast of Turkey. "I, John, your brother and fellow partaker in the *tribulation* and *kingdom* and *perseverance* which are in Jesus, was on the island called Patmos because of the word of God and the testimony of Jesus" (Rev. 1:9). He puts all the elements together—*tribulation, kingdom,* and *perseverance.* We have to make it through tribulations to the kingdom, and it will take perseverance!

This pattern is pronounced in the book of Revelation as a whole. *Tribulation* consisting of darkness, death, destruction and disaster unparalleled in human history is recorded. Uncounted numbers of saints *persevere* in the midst of this terrible tribulation. The *kingdom* envisioned by saints through the centuries is presented in almost unimaginable splendor in the final two chapters.

First John 3:2–3 helps pinpoint why the coming of Christ is such an important focal point for us: "Now we are children of God, and it has not appeared as yet what we will be. We know that when He appears, we will be like Him, because we will see Him just as He is. And everyone who has this hope fixed on Him purifies himself, just as He is pure."

Note the progression that John describes. First, we are children of God now. Our book is written to those who are children of God *now.* Second, we don't know exactly what it will be like when we are inducted into this future kingdom. Third, we do know, however, that we will become like Christ when He appears. Fourth, we will see Him as He is, and this in itself will be transforming. Fifth and finally, we who have this hope fixed on Christ are purified for our life journey. This is what we are talking about—how our future presence with Christ *purifies us for our life journey now*. The second coming of Christ is far more than a theological concept. It is more than a debate between pretribulation rapturists and midtribulationists, posttribulation adherents, amillennialists, or the outdated postmillennial position. It is the fact that Jesus Christ is coming again. We are to share His glory, His image and the destiny that become ours at this time. Anticipating His coming helps to transform our thinking, expectation and perspective throughout our journey. Take away this hope and something will always be missing from the process of long-term change.

Note how beautifully this concept was integrated in the apostle Paul's life when he put it all together with his relationship to Thessalonian believers. "For who is our hope or joy or crown of exultation? Is it not even you, in the presence of our Lord Jesus at His coming? For you are our glory and joy" (1 Thess. 2:19–20). Paul's future hope related to the coming of Christ included the Thessalonians. His input into their lives and their response would be an aspect of the glory of his life! This was part of his *hope agenda*.

We compared this final section to a musical chord with the minimum three notes. Titus 2:13–14 sounds the final chord. It combines our future hope with who and what we should be now. We must be those who are "looking for the blessed hope and the appearing of the glory of our great God and Savior, Christ Jesus who gave Himself for us to redeem us from every lawless deed, and to purify for Himself a people for His own possession, zealous for good deeds." Not to pursue and prepare to the best of our ability and then persevere to the end and experience long-term change is inexcusable!

For Reflection and Discussion
1. Do you struggle with the idea of Christ's coming as something that is remote and not very real?
2. Look again at the verses on the return of Christ in this chapter. Which ones stand out and why?
3. Do you give sufficient attention to the fact that Jesus Christ will return and what this means to us as believers?
4. Write a very brief summary of what the second coming of Jesus means to you.

Conclusion

A Big Picture of Long-Term Change

Blake's story helps put an exclamation point on our exploration of long-term change. He is self-employed in his own specialized business-to-business market niche. He came to a personal relationship with Christ through a professional associate—marketplace evangelism! He was a successful editor, and his career and life in general were at a high when he was converted. He thought, "Things will go even better now that God is with me and will work for my good."

He was in for terrific surprises for which he was unprepared. About this same time, his wife's health fell apart. Cancer, organ transplant, pervasive depression and a love of life died. Likewise, their marriage was reduced to two people living in the same house. She disparaged his business, ate alone and lived more as an occupant of the same house than a wife.

He began his business about the same time an associate did. His friend's business prospered but Blake's didn't. This began almost two decades of heartbreak, rage, resentment, bitterness and uncontrollable anger. I met with him as his mentor during many of these years. We met monthly in a splendid restaurant and became fixtures at the same corner table.

At one of our earlier meetings in a North Shore Chicago hotel, he suddenly raised his hands and exclaimed, "I don't get why in the h—— God deals with me like this!" His resentment and rage followed familiar patterns. "God must take perverse pleasure in beating me down. Why does He permit my wife to have such severe, ongoing health problems? God seems to make sure that I will not prosper in my business like others I know. Why must my business life be so hard and stressful without relief? Why doesn't God take away my anger and resentment? I keep asking Him to do so. Why is my wife so irrational—she makes my life miserable so often and doesn't appreciate anything I do?"

About ten years after our hotel meeting, we decided to meet even though Blake warned against it. He was really angry, he said. We met in a more isolated area of our large restaurant. I didn't see it coming, but he became enraged with loud and uncontrolled expressions of his deep hurt that related particularly to his wife. What happened next shocked and touched me. A woman sitting behind us who was eating with a friend heard the conversation. She put her hand gently on his shoulder and quietly spoke words to comfort and encourage him.

During those years, I used all sorts of strategies with Blake. I prayed for and with him. We ransacked the Bible. We pursed the curriculum of the *Life Serve Mentoring Program*. I took time to share his pain while encouraging him to stay the course. On one occasion I said sharply, "Quit whining." I tried to give input into his business and encourage him that it supported him even though it had not brought wealth. We talked often of God's plan for his life—hard but wonderful. I once told him,

A Big Picture of Long-Term Change

"You can rant and rave at God all you want but you are not going anywhere."

I said on another, "Suppose you were married to one of the most beautiful women in Chicago. Every night she was waiting for you and told you that you were the most wonderful man she had ever met. That would be great, but it would leave you without a special opportunity. You have the possibility of developing a nobility of loving in the face of your deprivation as a husband that you would never have had if you had married the consummate *North Shore Nellie*."

During these years, Blake practiced much of what we talked about in this book. He was faithful in using Scripture on a daily basis and met God at a local Panera coffee and pastry shop. He stayed in church and looked for ways to serve. As a relational person, he sought out fellowship with other Christians, attended our retreats, and actively participated in a group of Christian business owners. He began to work on memorizing and reviewing Scripture. He was faithful and uncompromising in sharing the gospel when he could.

I felt like a failure. Why didn't my counsel and input solve anything? I kept coming back to the idea that Blake's current experience would not end where he was. I didn't have the answers and felt pretty foolish, but I knew that God called him, Blake had responded, and he wouldn't end with the epithet *stalled* placed over his life.

He moved his niche business to Arizona and we continued our meetings remotely. He found two groups comprised of marketplace Christians. He put plastic over the Bible verses he was working on and kept them at one end of his swimming pool so that he could review them as he swam his laps.

Several months after his move, I received a call from him. His voice was alive. He said, "I have been yammering for so long about how God is treating me and griping about my life." He went on to share his gratefulness without his normal litany of complaints. He had moved to the dry, warm climate in Arizona particularly for his wife's benefit. She was doing a little better. His business had taken a marked upturn.

I said, "Way to go Blake!" and prayed in my heart, "Lord, I knew what I knew all along! We are in it for the long haul with You even though much of our pilgrimage can be painful and troubled." Blake's story is a good place to conclude our exploration of long-term change in the Christian life. Maybe your story is not as troubled as Blake's or maybe it's more difficult. Like his, our stories can be raw, plagued with problems, and messy with a lot of loose ends. Blake is still open about his heartaches and the unresolved issues in his life, but changes that eluded him for years are also his life realities that shine through the ongoing difficulties he faces.

A final footnote gets to the heart of Blake's story. During our last mentoring session, he mentioned hearing a famous radio Bible teacher say that he asked the Lord to glorify Himself in his life and at his expense. To my surprise, he said that he was beginning to pray that prayer himself. At his own admission, Blake's normal tendency is to be self-absorbed, easily frustrated, and prone to instant gratification. Why would he ever ask for something at his expense? This is where long-term change led him during his trouble-plagued Christian life. Little did he know that this is exactly what God had been doing for years in his experience as a follower of Christ. Had he been given everything he wanted when he wanted it as a believer, he would likely be a shadow of who he is today. At Blake's expense and for God's glory, he has achieved spiritual stature and maturity unavailable and impossible without the pain, discouragement, and deprivation deeply interwoven into his life. He did not isolate himself but shared, lamented, raged, and called out in his need within the company of fellow believers all along his way.

We too are not alone. We can share our pilgrimage with other Christians who love and support us. First Peter speaks of a great worldwide fellowship of believers who are enduring trials. We noted in an earlier chapter that God is with us as we struggle along. He is able to finish the work He started with us (Phil.1:6). The finish line is out in front of us. We are going to be like Christ, His closest relatives in another venue (Rom. 8:29). We will be perfected so that we can be presented to Christ like a bride "in all her glory, having no spot or wrinkle or any such thing; but that she would be holy and blameless" (Eph. 5:27).

The Holy Island of Lindisfarne off the northeast coast of England has a rich history. A line of poles across the tidal flats led pilgrims to the island. Still today, you have to keep moving so that you don't get caught in a high tide.

We are not moving toward Lindisfarne, home of the great Celtic leaders Aidan and Cuthbert in the seventh century. Rather, we travel toward the New Jerusalem described for us in Revelation 21–22. Like the pilgrims, we must keep moving. Our signposts along the way are not our destination. Victories, triumphs or transformative experiences tell us we are progressing. However, we are not to stop and erect a little chapel on the tidal flats of our lives to commemorate them. "Keep moving, you are not there yet" is the word for us.

We have every reason to persevere until we have achieved the last of the long-term changes that have stretched out in from of us during the course of our lives. Paul notes in 2 Timothy 4:7 that he came to a time in his life when he said, "I have fought the good fight, I have finished the course, I have kept the faith." "Go and do likewise" is our challenge (Luke 10:37 NIV). He added, "The Lord will . . . bring me safely to His heavenly kingdom" (2 Tim. 4:18). Let's continue—all the way.

For Reflection and Discussion

1. What is your bottom line now that you have considered *long-term change in a quick-fix world?*
2. Are you okay with this bigger picture of the Christian life and the long-term outlook that is required?
3. Which chapters are particularly relevant to you?
4. Use the chapters you selected and add others if you wish. Summarize the chapters you selected in a sentence or two to help keep the message in mind.

Bibliography

Briggs, Helen. "Plants 'Do Maths' to Control Overnight Food Supplies." BBC News, June 23, 2013, http://www.bbc.com/news/health-22991838.

Calhoun, Adele Ahlberg. *Spiritual Disciplines Handbook: Practices That Transform Us.* Downers Grove, IL: InterVarsity Press, 2005.

Caraway, Kenneth. "Boxed In, But Not Out," *Alive Now!* (March/April 1974): 14–15.

Chambers, Oswald. *Studies in the Sermon on the Mount.* 4th ed. London: Simpkin, Marshall, 1929.

Colson, Chuck. *Born Again.* Old Tappan, NJ: Revell, 1978.

Demarest, Bruce. *Satisfy Your Soul: Restoring the Heart of Christian Spirituality.* Colorado Springs: NavPress, 1999.

Discovery. Scripture Union. http://www.scriptureunion.org/Bible%20Reading/Discovery. Devotional guide for finding practical help from the Bible.

Edman, V. Raymond. *The Disciplines of Life.* Eugene, OR: Harvest House Publishers, 1982.

Farrar, Steve. *Finishing Strong: Going the Distance for Your Family.* Sisters, OR: Multnomah, 1995.

Finley, James. *Christian Meditation: Experiencing the Presence of God; A Guide to Contemplation.* San Francisco: HarperSanFrancisco, 2004.

Foster, Richard J. *Celebration of Discipline: The Path to Spiritual Growth.* San Francisco: Harper & Row, 1988.

Gladwell, Malcolm. *Outliers: The Story of Success.* New York: Little, Brown and Co., 2008.

Haley, Charles. "Healing and Restoration." In *Life Serve Mentoring Program.* Rev. ed. Wheaton: Life Serve, 2009. Originally published 2001.

Hendrix, Harville. *Getting the Love You Want: A Guide for Couples.* New York: Harper Perennial, 1988.

Inge, William Ralph. *Personal Religion and the Life of Devotion.* New York, London: Longmans, Green and Co., 1924.

Lao, Tzu. *The Way of Lao Tzu: Tao-Te Ching.* Translated, with introductory essays, comments, and notes by Wing-Tsit Chan. Indianapolis: Bobbs-Merrill, 1963.

McAlpine, Campbell. *The Practice of Biblical Meditation: Discovering a Deeper Spirituality through the Bible.* Tonbridge, England: Sovereign World, 2002. Originally published: London: Marshall Morgan & Scott, 1981. Page citations are to the Sovereign World edition.

Mulholland, Robert. *Invitation to a Journey: A Road Map for Spiritual Formation.* Downers Grove, IL: InterVarsity Press, 1985.

Noonan, Peggy. "There Is No Time, There Will Be Time." *Forbes ASAP,* November 30, 1998, reposted September 18, 2001, by *The Wall Street Journal,* http://online.wsj.com/news/articles/SB122409083174236943.

Nouwen, Henri J. M. *The Living Reminder: Service and Prayer in Memory of Jesus Christ.* San Francisco: HarperSanFrancisco,

1998. Originally published: New York: Seabury Press, 1977. Page citations are to the HarperSanFrancisco edition.

———. *The Return of the Prodigal Son: A Story of Homecoming.* London: Darton, Longman and Todd, 1992.

Our Daily Bread. RBC Ministries (formerly Radio Bible Class). http://odb.org/. Devotional distributed worldwide that helps readers spend time each day in God's Word. Available via print, large-print, radio, podcast, email, RSS, and mobile.

Rendall, T. S. *In God's School: Scriptural Studies Dealing with Various Disciplines Employed by God in the Training of His Children.* Three Hills, AB, Canada: Prairie Press, 1971.

Rohr, Richard. *Falling Upward: A Spirituality for the Two Halves of Life.* San Francisco: Jossey-Bass, 2011.

Seamands, David A. *Healing for Damaged Emotions.* Wheaton: Victor Books, 1981.

Taylor, Howard, and Mary Geraldine Taylor. *Hudson Taylor's Spiritual Secret.* London: China Inland Mission, 1932.

Toon, Peter. *From Mind to Heart: Christian Meditation Today.* Grand Rapids: Baker, 1987.

Underhill, Evelyn. *Mysticism: A Study in the Nature and Development of Spiritual Consciousness.* Mineola, NY: Dover Publications, 2002. Originally published: New York: E. P. Dutton, 1930. Page references are to the Dover edition.

Whitney, Donald S. *Spiritual Disciplines for the Christian Life.* Colorado Springs: NavPress, 1991.

Willard, Dallas. *The Spirit of the Disciplines: Understanding How God Changes Lives.* San Francisco: HarperSanFrancisco, 1990. First published 1988. Page references are to the 1990 edition.

Yousafzai, Malala, with Christina Lamb. *I Am Malala: The Girl Who Stood Up for Education and Was Shot by the Taliban.* London: London: Little, Brown and Co., 2013.

About the Author

Charles Haley is the founder of Life Serve, serving business owners and leaders through mentoring and life coaching (LifeServeLtd.com). After graduating from the University of Illinois, he earned a master of theology from Dallas Theological Seminary and a doctor of ministry from Northern Theological Seminary. Prior to starting Life Serve, Charles served as a college instructor, academic dean of students, pastor, and staff member of Fellowship of Companies for Christ International. He is the author of several books including *Beyond Leadership to Destiny*, *An Evangelical's Road Less Traveled*, *Dying to Live*, and *Praise in the Time Stream of Our Lives*. Charles and his wife, Jo Ann, live in Wheaton, Illinois. They are blessed with four married children and a large number of grandchildren and great-grandchildren.

About Life Serve

The mission of Life Serve is to help Christian leaders in the marketplace reach life goals spiritually, professionally, and personally.

Clients are served through a broad range of services anchored by the mentoring process. Mentoring "brings a range of gifts, skills, and materials within a program for spiritual growth and life formation" (Leech).

Listening, addressing the big issues that determine success or failure, and providing leveraged opportunities for spiritual formation and life development characterize the *Life Serve Mentoring Program.*

Visit Life Serve on the web at www.LifeServeLtd.com or contact Charles Haley at cwh@churchbuilding.com.